الملك

The Kingdom of God

A FULLY ILLUSTRATED COMMENTARY ON SURAH AL-MULK

ASIM KHAN

Foreword by
Mufti Menk

The Kingdom of God: A Fully Illustrated Commentary on Sūrah Al-Mulk

First published in England by
The Islamic Foundation
Markfield Conference Centre
Ratby Lane, Markfield
Leicestershire, LE67 9SY
United Kingdom
Tel: +44 (0) 1530 249230

Quran House, PO Box 30611, Kenya

P.M.B 3193 Kano, Nigeria

Website: www.kubepublishing.com
Email: info@kubepublishing.com

2nd impression, 2023

Cataloguing in-Publication Data is available from the British Library

ISBN Paperback 978-0-86037-865-5
ISBN Ebook 978-0-86037-870-9

Cover Design and Chapter Dividers: Mukhtar Sanders, Inspiral Design
Typesetting: Nasir Cadir
Graphics and Tables: Moghal Graphics
Stock Images: Pixabay and Wikipedia

Printed by: Elma Basim, Turkey

Contents

Acknowledgements

Our beloved Prophet Muḥammad ﷺ taught us that "Whoever has not thanked people, has not thanked Allāh".

I am honoured to have studied the commentary of this chapter of the Qur'ān with my mentor and esteemed teacher Shaykh Dr Haitham al-Haddād. I am forever indebted to him for instilling within me the love of the Qur'ān and the burning desire to share its message with those around me.

Thank you to my wife Sobia Akram for your continued love and support. More gratitude than can be expressed goes to my mother and father who raised me well, loved me and taught me to aim high.

My four beautiful daughters. My dream is to see you grow to become scholars of the Qur'ān who commit themselves to a life-long study of its meanings and teach its message to the world.

Foreword by Mufti Menk

All praise is due to Almighty Allāh, and peace and blessings be upon His final Messenger Muḥammad ﷺ.

The Qur'ān is the source of light for humanity. Unless we spend our lives reading it, studying its meanings, and reflecting over its verses, we will never fully expose ourselves to this vital light and its all-encompassing guidance and benefits.

This book, suitably titled 'The Kingdom of God', delves into the profound meanings and guidance found in *Sūrah al-Mulk,* the 67th chapter of the Qur'ān. It contains key features that are unique for a book explaining a chapter of the Qur'ān, such as the diagrams and illustrations highlighting the beautiful meanings of the verses.

Readers are also introduced to the works of the earliest scholars written in an easy-to-understand language.

The reader is taken on a captivating journey that explores diverse topics, including tenets of faith, political issues, spirituality, and social affairs, in a smooth and coherent manner.

Unlike many books of the same genre translated into English from Arabic, the present work is written by an English-speaking author who was raised in the UK and studied the Islamic sciences in Cairo, Egypt.

I ask Almighty Allāh to grant the distinguished author, Ustadh Asim Khan, greater acceptance.

May Almighty Allāh bless his family, students, and friends who have supported him throughout his journey of writing '*The Kingdom of God*', *Āmīn*.

Mufti Menk
Harare, Zimbabwe
Aug 2021/1442

The Central Message of *Sūrah al-Mulk*

Each chapter (*Sūrah*) of the Qur'ān has its own unique features, which leave a special impression on the reader. This *Sūrah* takes its name, **al-Mulk**, from its very first verse. As well as being called **al-Mulk (the Kingdom)**, it is also known as ***al-Wāqiyah***[1] (the Protector), ***al-Munjiyah***[2] (the Rescuer), and ***al-Māniʿah*** (the Defender) because it protects the one who recites it and rescues them from the punishment of the grave.[3] It is also called ***al-Mujādilah*** (the Advocate) because it advocates on behalf of the one who recites it upon being interrogated in the grave.[4]

Sūrah al-Mulk speaks about Allāh, the Creator, in a way that makes the heart feel His presence. It outlines an array of emotions and manners that a person should strive to internalise in order to place his Maker at the centre of his life. The overall message is succinctly captured within its opening verse: *Blessed is the One in whose Hands rests the Kingdom. And He is Most Capable of everything*. The *Sūrah* challenges the reader to formulate a new concept of the universe and its relationship with its Creator as being like that of a kingdom with respect to a king. A number of frightening warnings are given to awaken those who are spiritually lost; promises of punishment are delivered to those bent on disbelief.

1 *Al-Jāmiʿ li-Aḥkām al-Qur'ān*, by al-Qurṭubī. See introduction to *Sūrah al-Mulk*.

2 Ibid.

3 Ibn ʿAbbās said, 'A man from amongst the Companions of the Prophet ﷺ erected a tent over a grave without realising. Then, behold, *Sūrah al-Mulk* was [heard] being recited from the grave until it was completed. The man came to the Prophet ﷺ saying, "O Messenger of Allāh! I erected a tent above a grave without realising only to hear *Sūrah al-Mulk* being recited in its entirety". The Prophet ﷺ said, "Truly it is al-Māniʿah (the Defender), truly it is al-Munjiyah (the Rescuer), rescuing the person from the punishment of the grave"'. [Reported in *Sunan* of al-Tirmidhī]

4 *Tafsīr Al-Taḥrīr wa al-Tanwīr*, Ibn ʿĀshūr. See introduction to *Sūrah al-Mulk*.

Sūrah al-Mulk invites the reader to look at how the universe is moved by God's Will, under His perfect control. It speaks of creatures living on earth alongside man, such as the *jinn* and the birds, or other matters belonging to the Afterlife, such as hell and its keepers. The reader is sent on a journey to discover a new sense of perspective about the power of God and the extent of His control over the cosmos and beyond. From this newfound enlightened viewpoint, the planet and the present worldly life pale into insignificance when placed before the vastness of the seven heavens and the eternity of the Afterlife.

Figure 1: Depiction of the Ka'bah during the early Ottoman period

The revelation of the Qur'ān can be divided into Makkan and Madinan *Suwar* (plural of 'Sūrah'). The Makkan *Suwar* were revealed over the course of 13 years before the migration of the Prophet ﷺ to the city of Madinah, and the Madinan *Suwar* were revealed thereafter.

The Makkan *Suwar* have distinct characteristics in that their focus is on developing a purely monotheistic faith and a worldview centred on the Afterlife. Revelations of the Madinan era provide details on how to implement such beliefs, standards, and values in practical everyday life. *Sūrah al-Mulk* is a classic example of a Makkan *Sūrah*.[5] It seeks to strengthen and fortify the faith of the believers, and to develop the foundations upon which Allāh's commands and prohibitions rest.

In terms of a timeline, even though *Sūrah al-Mulk* is the 67th chapter of the Qur'ān, it was the 76th in the chronology of revelation during the life of the Prophet ﷺ.[6] Imām Ibn ʿĀshūr states that it was revealed after *Sūrah al-Mu'minūn* and before *al-Ḥāqqah*. On the basis of a report in which ʿUmar b. al-Khaṭṭāb said that *Sūrah al-Ḥāqqah* was revealed five years before the migration,[7] i.e. in the 8th year of Prophecy, it is possible to date the revelation of *Sūrah al-Mulk* to the 7th or 8th year of the Makkan era. The following timeline illustrates this.

---

5 *Al-Jāmiʿ li-Aḥkām al-Qurʾān*, by al-Qurṭubī. See introduction of *Sūrah al-Mulk*.

6 *Tafsīr Al-Taḥrīr wa Al-Tanwīr*, Ibn ʿĀshūr. See introduction to *Sūrah al-Mulk*.

7 Ibid, *Tafsīr Al-Taḥrīr wa Al-Tanwīr*, Ibn ʿĀshūr. See introduction to *Sūrah al-Mulk*.

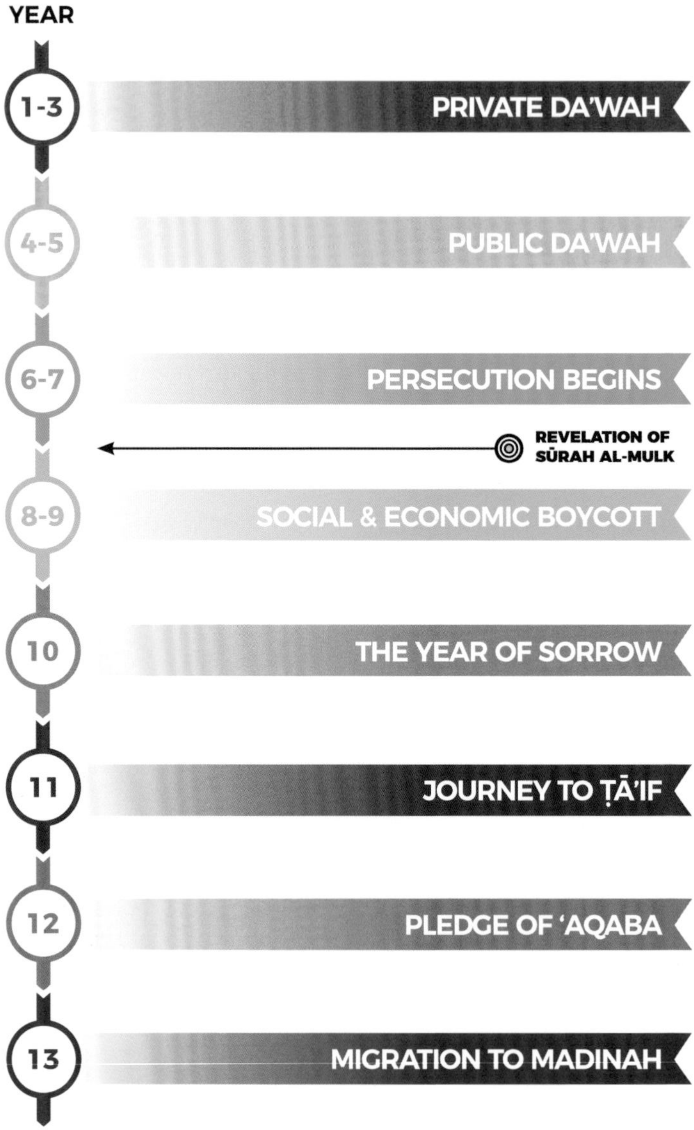

Figure 2: Timeline of the Makkan Era & revelation of Sūrah al-Mulk

19 Descriptions of God in *Sūrah al-Mulk*

Sūrah al-Mulk speaks about Allāh, the Creator, in a way that makes the heart feel His presence. It outlines an array of emotions and manners that a person should strive to internalise in order to place his Maker at the centre of his life. The *Sūrah* introduces the reader to many Names and Attributes of Allāh, the Almighty, which highlight His sublime power and the extent of His control. Here is a list of 19 descriptions of God that we can find in the *Sūrah*:

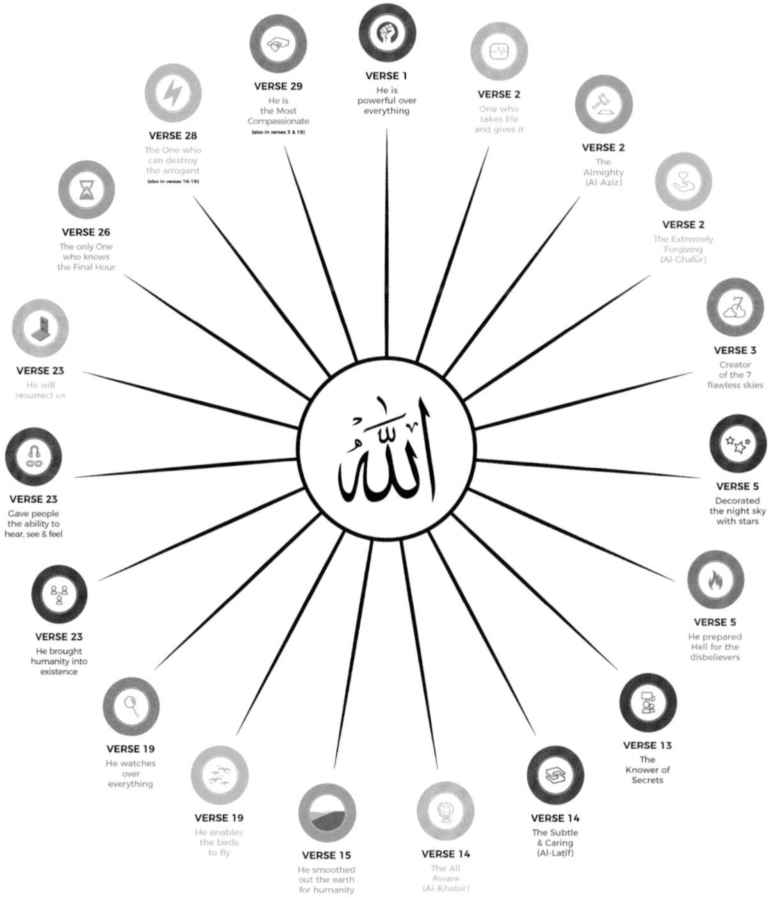

Figure 3: The 19 attributes of God mentioned in Sūrah al-Mulk

Thematic Breakdown of *Sūrah al-Mulk*

The following thematic breakdown of *Sūrah al-Mulk* shows that it contains six distinct core sections, each covering a different theme. However, upon closer examination, one can observe that the *Sūrah* has a lineal progression and a symmetrical coherence. This is part and parcel of the eloquence of the Qur'ān and its miraculous nature.

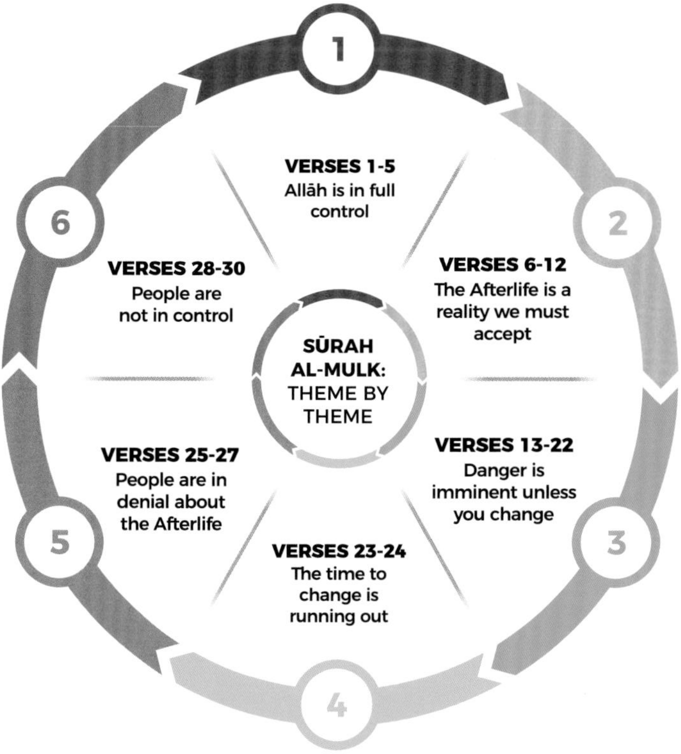

Figure 4: Thematic breakdown of Sūrah al-Mulk

Figure 5: Signs of symmetry between the 6 sections of Sūrah al-Mulk

The Sources

The sources from the Qur'ānic commentary literature (*tafsīr*) that are highlighted throughout the book can be seen below:

Of all the books I consulted, I relied heavily on the work of Shaykh al-Ṭāhir ibn 'Āshūr, which formed the basis of this commentary. I also relied on the work of the Andalusian Imām al-Qurṭubī. Then, I searched for as many linguistic and spiritually uplifting points of benefit. Many of these were found in the brilliant works of al-Rāzī, al-Ālūsī, and al-Zamakhsharī. I also stumbled upon many marvellous subtleties in the works of Dr. Fāḍil al-Sāmarā'ī, which I have tried to include. Collectively, the research behind this book draws upon scholarly works spanning over a thousand years.

BOOK	AUTHOR	DEATH (H/AD)	NO. OF TIMES CITED
Tafsīr al-Qurʾān al-ʿaẓīm	ʿImād al-Dīn Abu'l-Fidāʾ Ismāʿīl ibn ʿUmar ibn Kathīr	774 | 1373	22
Jāmiʿ al-bayān ʿan taʾwīl āy al-Qurʾān	Muḥammad ibn Jarīr al-Ṭabarī	310 | 923	21
al-Jāmiʿ li-aḥkām al-Qurʾān	Abū ʿAbd Allāh Muḥammad ibn Aḥmad al-Qurṭubī	671 | 1272	16
al-Taḥrīr wa'l-tanwīr	Muḥammad al-Ṭāhir ibn ʿĀshūr	1393 | 1973	15
Rūḥ al-maʿānī fī tafsīr al-Qurʾān al-ʿaẓīm wa'l-sabʿ al-mathānī	Shihāb al-Dīn al-Ālūsī	1270 | 1854	12
al-Tafsīr al-kabīr, also known as Mafātīḥ al-ghayb	Fakhr al-Dīn al-Rāzī	606 | 1210	8
al-Kashshāf ʿan ghawāmiḍ ḥaqāʾiq al-tanzīl wa ʿuyūn al-aqāwīl fī wujūh al-taʾwīl	Abu'l-Qāsim Maḥmūd ibn ʿUmar al-Zamakhsharī	538 | 1144	4
al-Muḥarrar al-wajīz fī tafsīr al-kitāb al-ʿazīz	Abū Muḥammad ʿAbd al-Ḥaqq ibn ʿAṭiyyah al-Andalusī	541 | 1147	3
Naẓm al-durar fī tanāsub al-āyāt wa'l-suwar	Burhān al-Dīn Abu'l-Ḥasan Ibrāhīm al-Biqāʿī	885 | 1480	3

الملك

Section One

Verses 1–5

Allah is Powerful

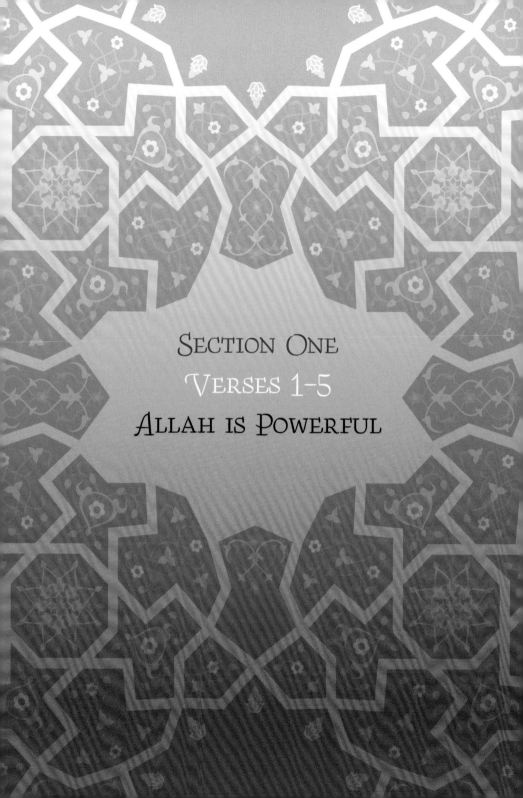

Section One [Verses 1–5]

Allah is Powerful

Section one sets the scene for the rest of the *Sūrah*. It begins by speaking about the Almighty as being the source of abundant goodness which manifests itself in the world around us. With this positive image of God in mind, we are told He is in charge of the entire universe, has control over our lives, and has designed this life as a test to see which of us rise to the challenges with faith and conviction.

Section one ends by speaking about the signs of God in nature and, in particular, the flawlessness of the sky and the beauty of the stars. We are told about how, in the spiritual world, there are devils who try to eavesdrop on the conversations taking place between angels in the heavens. All of these details point towards the power of Allāh over His Kingdom, both in the physical world as well as in the spiritual world.

Section One Verses 1–5
Allah is Powerful

1. Blessed is the One in Whose Hands rests the Kingdom. And He is Most Capable of everything.	تَبَارَكَ الَّذِي بِيَدِهِ الْمُلْكُ وَهُوَ عَلَىٰ كُلِّ شَيْءٍ قَدِيرٌ ﴿١﴾
2. [He is the One] Who created death and life in order to test which of you is better in deeds. And He is the Almighty, The Extremely Forgiving.	الَّذِي خَلَقَ الْمَوْتَ وَالْحَيَاةَ لِيَبْلُوَكُمْ أَيُّكُمْ أَحْسَنُ عَمَلًا ۚ وَهُوَ الْعَزِيزُ الْغَفُورُ ﴿٢﴾
3. [He is the One] Who created seven heavens, one above the other. You will never see any imperfection in the creation of the Most Compassionate. So look again: do you see any flaws?	الَّذِي خَلَقَ سَبْعَ سَمَاوَاتٍ طِبَاقًا ۖ مَّا تَرَىٰ فِي خَلْقِ الرَّحْمَٰنِ مِن تَفَاوُتٍ ۖ فَارْجِعِ الْبَصَرَ هَلْ تَرَىٰ مِن فُطُورٍ ﴿٣﴾
4. Then look again and again – your sight will return frustrated and weary.	ثُمَّ ٱرْجِعِ ٱلْبَصَرَ كَرَّتَيْنِ يَنقَلِبْ إِلَيْكَ ٱلْبَصَرُ خَاسِئًا وَهُوَ حَسِيرٌ ﴿٤﴾
5. And indeed, We adorned the lowest heaven with [stars like] lamps, and made them [as missiles] for stoning [eavesdropping] devils, for whom We have also prepared the torment of the Blaze.	وَلَقَدْ زَيَّنَّا السَّمَاءَ الدُّنْيَا بِمَصَابِيحَ وَجَعَلْنَاهَا رُجُومًا لِّلشَّيَاطِينِ ۖ وَأَعْتَدْنَا لَهُمْ عَذَابَ السَّعِيرِ ﴿٥﴾

تَبَارَكَ الَّذِى بِيَدِهِ الْمُلْكُ وَهُوَ عَلَىٰ كُلِّ شَىْءٍ قَدِيرٌ ﴿١﴾

1. Blessed is the One in Whose Hands rests the Kingdom. And He is Most Capable of everything.

The Polytheists of Makkah would claim that there were other gods out there who could control people's fate, grant them blessings, and intercede on their behalf before the Almighty. This was the dominant belief-system and worldview of the Arabs when the Prophet ﷺ first began his mission in 610 CE. He, along with a small band of followers, were a persecuted minority whose religious beliefs were ridiculed and shut down. Despite total authority being in the hands of the Quraysh, Allāh revealed *Sūrah al-Mulk* declaring: **Blessed is the One in Whose Hands rests the Kingdom**. Reciting this in public would have been seen as a challenge to the political powers of that time.

The first word *tabāraka* comes from the same root as *barakah,* often translated as 'blessings', but more accurately refers to the idea of something having extraordinary goodness beyond expectation.[8] The accomplishments of the Prophet ﷺ is a glaring example of *barakah.* In the words of Thomas Carlyle—one the most important social commentators of his time—"how one man single-handedly could bring together warring tribes and Bedouins into the most powerful and civilised nation in less than two decades is an enigma (mystery)?" This is part of the meaning of *tabāraka,* to be the source of *barakah*—extraordinary goodness—and have the power to infuse and instil this into others. Another aspect of the meaning, as highlighted by the Tunisian scholar Ibn ʿĀshūr, is of manifesting or displaying this quality.[9] For instance, a king who has great power but never exercises it will not be referred to as a powerful king. Allāh not only has the quality of being the source of all goodness, but He manifests that throughout His kingdom such

8 *Tafsīr Al-Taḥrīr wa Al-Tanwīr,* Ibn ʿĀshūr 67:1, Ibn ʿĀshūr.
9 Ibid.

that His creation recognises and appreciates that about Him. Piecing these meanings together, we learn that *tabāraka* means that Allāh is the source of all goodness, a type of goodness that is vast and extreme, constantly being instilled into the world around us to varying degrees. This meaning can be confirmed through another verse of the Qur'ān in which the Almighty says: *Blessed is the One Who sent down the Standard to His servant*[10] for by sending down the 'Standard', i.e., the Qur'ān, did He display His goodness to mankind in the most sensational and obvious way possible.

The words **in Whose Hands rests the Kingdom**[11] have been explained by the great Qur'ānic exegete, Ibn Kathīr, to mean that Allāh is governing the affairs of all creation in whichever manner He chooses without anyone being able to challenge His rule or question His actions.[12] Specifically, the word *mulk*, translated here as Kingdom, encapsulates the meaning of being the supreme authority, having a dominion to rule over, and wielding power over it. This, as Ibn Kathīr explains, segues neatly into the end of the verse **And He is Most Capable of everything**.

Rhetorical Devices

The statement **in Whose Hands rests the Kingdom** is made more powerful through the use of three rhetorical devices:

1. The sequence of the word flow has been altered to literally read 'in His hand lies the Kingdom', whereas the simpler sequence would have been 'the Kingdom lies in His Hand'. According to Ibn ʿĀshūr, this creates exclusivity in the meaning, as if to say the Kingdom lies solely in God's Hand and no one else's.[13]

10 Qur'ān 25:1

11 According to Ibn ʿĀshūr, the letter *ba* in the word *bi-yadihi* can also be interpreted to mean 'because', as if to say: the reason why Allāh is able to direct His blessings to wherever He wishes is because the whole kingdom is in His Hand.

12 *Tafsīr al-Qur'ān al-ʿAẓīm* 67:1, Ibn Kathīr.

13 *Tafsīr Al-Taḥrīr wa Al-Tanwīr* 67:1, Ibn ʿĀshūr.

2. According to Imām al-Zamakhsharī, the word *yad*, translated as 'hand', is used metaphorically to express total control, power, and dominance.[14]

3. The use of the definite noun *al-mulk* with the *alif-lām*, as opposed to *mulk*, creates an all-encompassing meaning, as if to say that He is in control of every part of the kingdom and that every individual is within His Grasp. All of them are under His authority, being provided for and bound by Him.

We can now attempt to highlight these nuances through a modified translation.

ORIGINAL TRANSLATION

> Blessed is the One in Whose Hands rests the Kingdom. And He is Most Capable of everything

VS.

MODIFIED TRANSLATION

> Blessed **beyond limit** is the One in Whose Hands rests **entirely and exclusively** the Kingdom. And He is Most Capable of everything

14 *al-Kashshāf* 67:1, al-Zamakhsharī.

The verse ends with a frequently mentioned statement in the Qur'ān: **And He is Most Capable of everything**. Ibn ʿĀshūr explained this statement as being a generaliser that broadens the meaning to include what could be missed out of the previous statement **in Whose Hands rests the Kingdom**.[15] There, Allāh spoke in particular about being in control of this kingdom which is then expanded to include that which lies beyond the kingdom of this universe, as well as what exists in the spiritual world. The last word of the verse *qadīr* comes from the root word *qadar,* which means to determine, decree, and to have ability; all these meanings revolve around the idea of being able to restrict and limit.

The overall message of this phrase could serve as a rebuttal to all those who ascribe power and control to any other than Allāh, such as the polytheists with their belief in the idols.

The Beginning & End

The beginning and end of the verse beautifully contrast with one another. The beginning is about Allāh being the source of all goodness, goodness which is great and vast, and the ending of the verse states that everything other than Him falls under His decree and limits (*qadr*). The infinite abundance of Allāh's goodness is thus elevated further by contrasting it with the limited nature of the human experience.

15 *Al-Taḥrīr wa Al-Tanwīr* 67:1, Ibn ʿĀshūr.

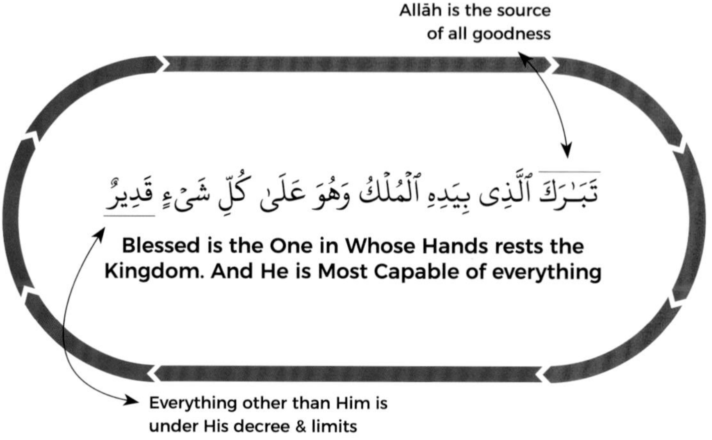
Allāh is the source of all goodness
تَبَـٰرَكَ ٱلَّذِى بِيَدِهِ ٱلْمُلْكُ وَهُوَ عَلَىٰ كُلِّ شَىْءٍ قَدِيرٌ
Blessed is the One in Whose Hands rests the Kingdom. And He is Most Capable of everything
Everything other than Him is under His decree & limits

Figure 6: The contrast in meaning between the beginning and ending of verse 1

Reflection

The great Companion, Ibn ʿAbbās, alluded to the consequences of believing that Allāh is **the One in Whose Hands rests the Kingdom.** He said, '[Allāh] elevates whoever He wishes and disgraces whoever He wishes, He gives life and takes it, He enriches and impoverishes, and He grants and deprives.'[16] Therefore, this one idea of Allāh's Kingship produces many others, namely, the belief that our fate, our happiness, and escape from misery is all with Him alone.

16 *Al-Jāmiʿ li-Aḥkām al-Qurʾān* 67:1, by al-Qurṭubī.

ٱلَّذِى خَلَقَ ٱلْمَوْتَ وَٱلْحَيَوٰةَ لِيَبْلُوَكُمْ أَيُّكُمْ أَحْسَنُ عَمَلًا ۚ
وَهُوَ ٱلْعَزِيزُ ٱلْغَفُورُ ﴿٢﴾

2. [He is the One] Who created death and life in order to test which of you is better in deeds. And He is the Almighty, The Extremely Forgiving.

Having power over someone's life demonstrates having absolute control and authority over them. Being able to bring something to life from nothing and shape its growth, development, and fate serves only to elevate that authority further into the realm of divinity and instils a sense of indebtedness in the one gifted with life. This is what **[He is the One] Who created death and life** means. Allāh alone holds such capability and power.[17]

From our human perspective, a scenario in which someone gains control over another person's life is usually a tyrannical one, perhaps a case of ransom or blackmail. The person takes advantage of that power and uses it for their own interests and benefit. So how then does God use His power? The verse explains that the Almighty's power and control over humanity is not used against them but rather used **to test which of you is better in deeds**.

Life and death are two familiar phenomena. Yet the verse invites us to look at what lies beyond these two phenomena of God's Will, Wisdom, and the way He sets tests and conducts all affairs.

17 *Naẓm al-Durar* 67:2, al-Biqāʿī.

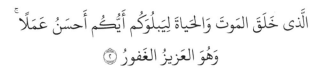

What is the link between verse 1 & 2?

Scholars that focus on coherence in the Qur'ān point out that the first verse speaks about Allāh's power and authority in a general sense, captured in the words **in Whose Hands rests the Kingdom**, and thereafter specific insight is provided into how much control He has over humanity and their affairs.[18] This is the extent of Allāh's Kingship—He not only holds authority over the universe, but the life that exists within it is also under His complete control. Can any king of this world rival that? In fact, even the greatest kings in history who enjoyed the love and loyalty of their people all feared the one thing they had no control over: death.

People hardly ever look beyond their immediate life or think of a world beyond what they can see and touch. They are, so to say, locked within the cage of their current life on earth. This verse encourages the reader to break through this restrictive paradigm.

[He is the One] Who created death and life in order to test which of you is better in deeds. Though many translate the Arabic word *aḥsan* as 'best' it can also mean 'better'. The phrase would thus mean that Allāh tests people to give them a chance to do better; to improve, to develop, to move closer to Him. This idea of doing better resonates with the human soul as every person desires to become the best version of themselves. Another difference in meaning between 'better' and 'best' is that the idea of being better shifts the focus from the outcome to the process. For instance, if there was a race and the commentator was asked "who was the best player" and then asked "who did better", he may give three different answers, as "better" could describe one who improved the most or worked the hardest or overcame the most adversities.

18 *Rūḥ al-Maʿānī fī Tafsīr al-Qur'ān al-ʿĀẓīm wa'l-Sabʿ al-Mathānī* 67:2, by al-Ālūsī.

The Arabic word 'to test you' is *ibtilā'*. Its core meaning revolves around the idea of testing, examining, and putting to trial. The word *ibtilā'* is also the hyperbolised spelling of the word *balā'*, which intensifies the meaning[19] as if to say the tests of life will be thorough and ongoing. The first part of the verse is, therefore, explaining that Allāh has intentionally designed life to be one in which people will experience tests and challenges. Interestingly, the Qur'ān explains that these tests will come in the form of both fortune and misfortune. For instance, Allāh says elsewhere in the Qur'ān: *We test you [O humanity] with good and evil as a trial.* (*Al-Anbiyā* 21:35) The great king and Prophet Sulaymān was blessed with tremendous power, fame, and wealth. When he saw the Queen Sheba's throne stationed before him, he exclaimed: *This is by the grace of my Lord to test me whether I am grateful or ungrateful.* (*Al-Naml* 27:40)

The question then arises: why would God create life riddled with tests and adversity? This is immediately answered in the next part of the verse: it is in order to see **which of you is better in deeds.**

Better in terms of what?

The phrase **to test which of you is better in deeds** has been interpreted in a number of ways. It is said that upon reciting this *Sūrah*, the Prophet ﷺ stopped when he reached **which of you is better in deeds** and said, "The most wary of what God has forbidden and the quickest to obey God."[20] However, the narration is not considered to be authentic by many scholars and so other interpretations have been put forward:

1. Which of you is better in using their intellect.[21]
2. Which of you is better in being mindful of death and preparing for it.[22]

19 As explained by Dr Fāḍil al-Sāmarā'ī.
20 *Rūḥ al-Ma'ānī fī Tafsīr al-Qur'ān al-'Aẓīm wa'l-Sab' al-Mathānī* 67:2, by al-Ālūsī.
21 *Al-Kashshāf* 67:2, al-Zamakhsharī.
22 *Al-Jāmi' li-Aḥkām al-Qur'ān* 67:2, by al-Qurṭubī.

3. Better in obeying Allāh and being wary of violating His prohibitions.
4. Better in terms of sincerity and being more correct in terms of adhering to the Sunnah.[23]
5. Better in terms of being less worldly and materialistic.[24]

Finally, the word choice of 'better' instead of 'more' places an emphasis upon intention and sincerity. This is because, had Allāh said 'to see which of you does more good deeds', the focus would be more on quantity over quality.

Reflection

Trials are considered an aspect of God's Mercy since they are an integral part of the process of purification. When asked which human beings suffer the greatest trials, the Prophet ﷺ answered, "The prophets, then those most like them. A person is tested according to the level of his faith. If his faith is firm, his trials increase in severity, and if there is weakness in his faith, he will be tried accordingly."

The Two Names: The Almighty & The Extremely Forgiving

These two Names of Allāh conclude the verse and succinctly capture its message. Verse 2 informs humanity that Allāh is the One who controls their life and fate, and this is a result of Him being *al-ʿAzīz*, the Almighty. The verses also convey that life has been designed as a test to see who will rise to tribulation with faith, as Allāh wishes to grant humanity forgiveness and reward as He is *al-Ghafūr*, the Extremely Forgiving.

23 *Al-Kashshāf* 67:2, al-Zamakhsharī.

24 *Al-Muḥarrar al-Wajīz fī Tafsīr al-Kitāb al-ʿAzīz* 67:2, ibn ʿAṭiyyah al-Andalūsī.

These two Names of Allāh also tie into the idea of testing people. For instance, in order to be a judge at a competition, the person will need to have authority for their judgement to carry weight and be safe from being undermined. The verse describes Allāh as being *al-ʿAzīz*, which means to have power and dominance, but also implies having the power to punish those who neglected and failed the test of life. As for the believers, they are reminded that Allāh is *al-Ghafūr*, meaning the One who forgives and conceals people's mistakes. This serves to motivate them to pass the test of life as forgiveness will lead to Paradise. As Allāh says elsewhere, *'But I am truly Most Forgiving to whoever repents, believes, and does good, then persists on [true] guidance.'* [25]

Reflection

The combination of the Names 'The Almighty' and 'The Extremely Forgiving' has a stark contrast. The first invokes the idea of power, authority, and punishment, whereas the second invokes the idea of love, forgiveness, and kindness. A possible lesson that can be deduced is that a believer should not become complacent by taking Allāh's mercy to an extreme, nor should they become pessimistic about Allāh and their fate in the Afterlife. Rather, a believer should aspire to find the middle ground between these two evil extremes.

الَّذِى خَلَقَ سَبْعَ سَمَاوَاتٍ طِبَاقًا ۖ مَّا تَرَىٰ فِى خَلْقِ الرَّحْمَٰنِ مِن تَفَاوُتٍ ۖ
فَارْجِعِ الْبَصَرَ هَلْ تَرَىٰ مِن فُطُورٍ ﴿٣﴾

3. [He is the One] Who created seven heavens, one above the other. You will never see any imperfection in the creation of the Most Compassionate. So look again: do you see any flaws?

25 Qur'ān 20:82.

ثُمَّ ٱرۡجِعِ ٱلۡبَصَرَ كَرَّتَيۡنِ يَنقَلِبۡ إِلَيۡكَ ٱلۡبَصَرُ خَاسِئٗا وَهُوَ حَسِيرٞ ٤

4. Then look again and again – your sight will return frustrated and weary.

The description of Allāh and the extent of His dominance over the universe, as mentioned in verse 1, is now expanded upon in greater detail.[26] The human race is a small part of the whole cosmic system of matter and energy known as the universe. Despite its vastness in size, the universe represents just one sky (*samā'*) from the seven skies (*samāwāt*) in existence. In verse 3, the Qur'ān refers to them by saying: **[He is the One] Who created seven heavens, one above the other**.

People rarely look beyond the beautiful blue sky to see God's Hand that brought them into existence, or the perfection with which they manifest. The words **one above the other** literally means the seven skies are stacked on top of one another[27] such that where one ends, the other begins seamlessly with no gaps or unevenness.[28] This is why the next part of the verse says: **You will never see any imperfection in the creation of the Most Compassionate**.

Even though the word *tafāwut* has been translated as 'imperfection', it originally refers to the gap in between the fingers.[29] Other specialists in the Arabic language explain it to mean something that lacks proportion or balance such that parts of it fail to connect with other parts.[30] In the context of the verse, it means that even though the skies Allāh has created are separate entities, they are seamlessly connected in harmony.

26 *Tafsīr Al-Taḥrīr wa Al-Tanwīr* 67:3, Ibn ʿĀshūr.
27 *Jāmiʿ al-Bayān fī Ta'wīl al- Qur'ān* 67:3, Imām al-Ṭabarī.
28 *Al-Tafsīr Al-Kabīr* 67:3, *Al-Tafsīr al-Kabīr* 67:12, al-Rāzī.
29 *Al-Muʿjam al-Ishtiqāqī*, entry فوت, Muḥammad Ḥasan Jabal.
30 *Al-Taḥrīr wa Al-Tanwīr* 67:3, Ibn ʿĀshūr.

In fact, the wording of the verse expands the meaning to relate to all of God's creation, including nature, expressing a sense of proportion and fine-tuning which it exhibits. This is because the verse does not say 'You will never see any imperfection in the **skies**', but rather 'in the **creation**'. This creation is referred to as the **creation of the Most Compassionate** (*al-Raḥmān*), as if to say, the absence of imperfections in nature is a reflection of Allāh's mercy, care, and compassion for humanity.[31] He wants to facilitate life for them in an organised and orderly way. Observing nature then, even by watching a wildlife documentary, should be a spiritual experience that brings the soul closer to Allāh. Verse 3 then challenges the critic to spot any flaws through their own tools and not to take what is being said for granted: **So look again: do you see any flaws?** Here 'flaws' literally means cracks or gaping holes.[32]

Word choice

In verse 3, two words have been used that have similar meanings: imperfections (*tafāwut*) and flaws (*fuṭūr*). In English, the difference between the two is hardly noticeable, but in Arabic, the difference reveals the wisdom and perfection in Allāh's speech.

As for the word 'imperfections' (*tafāwut*), it comes from the root word *fawt*, which means a gap in between the fingers. The word 'flaws' (*fuṭūr*) comes from the root *faṭr* which refers to a hole made in the ground for a well. The difference between the two is that *tafāwut* refers to small gaps that are difficult to spot from a far-away distance, whereas the second word, *fuṭūr*, describes bigger gaps, large enough for a well to flow out of, which can thus be seen from a distance. Reading these details back into the verse can reveal a subtle point of benefit. The verse first stated that there are no imperfections (*tafāwut*) in nature and that if people were to examine nature themselves, they would not see any flaws (*fuṭūr*).

31 *Al-Taḥrīr wa Al-Tanwīr* 67:3, Ibn ʿĀshūr.

32 *Rūḥ al-Maʿānī fī Tafsīr al-Qur'ān al-ʿAẓīm wa'l-Sabʿ al-Mathānī* 67:3, by al-Ālūsī.

A possible reason for this could be that Allāh is demonstrating, through the choice of words, that whether you observe nature from a distance or under a microscope, you will never spot any imperfections.

Reflection

When we relate this concept of nature being an expression of Allāh's mercy to the previous verse about how life was created in order **to test** people, we can say that the tests and hardships Allāh decrees for people are also a manifestation of His mercy. This is because tests and trials are a part of Allāh creation, and are an integral part of the process of purification for a believer. When asked which human beings suffer the greatest trials, the Prophet ﷺ answered, "The prophets, then those most like them. A person is tested according to the level of his faith. If his faith is firm, his trials increase in severity, and if there is weakness in his faith, he will be tried accordingly." With regard to trials faced by believers, another *ḥadīth* says, "No fatigue, disease, sorrow, sadness, hurt, or distress befalls a Muslim—even if he be pricked by a thorn—but that God expiates some of his sins thereby."[33] In this sense, affliction can be considered a blessing for the opportunities it presents. Another *ḥadīth* says, "If God wants to do good to somebody, He afflicts him with trials."[34]

Verse 4 stresses the idea of God's creation being flawless. It urges the critic: **Then look again and again—your sight will return frustrated and weary,** where *karatayn* is to look over and over again.[35] This means that if there are those in doubt about God's existence and His right to be worshipped, they need only observe and study the world of nature, its design, organisation, and beauty, as this would cause them to realise certain spiritual truths which the soul finds difficult to deny.

33 *Ḥadīth, Ṣaḥīḥ al-Bukhārī* 5641.
34 *Ḥadīth, Ṣaḥīḥ al-Bukhārī* 5645.
35 *Al-Jāmiʿ li-Aḥkām al-Qur'ān* 67:4, by al-Qurṭubī.

The instruction to look over and over again also implies that the more humanity studies nature, the more details and wonders it will reveal to them, which, in turn, would create a deeper conviction for those with sincere hearts in the existence of Allāh.[36] On the contrary, when people repeatedly engage with manmade products, their appreciation and excitement diminishes the more they experience it. A typical example is when purchasing a new phone. Even if it is the latest model with cutting-edge technology, the novelty quickly begins to wear off and, upon closer inspection, the flaws of the product start to become noticeable.

Verse 4 ends with **your sight will return frustrated and weary**, which is referring to the eye that tries hard to find defects in God's creation. Such a person will become increasingly frustrated at the lack of flaws he wishes to find. It also means this person will experience, what one might when met with failure in their attempt to spot defects. The moment when an arrogant person who was convinced they were right realises they were completely wrong, this is the facial reaction being captured in the verse **your sight will return frustrated and weary**.

وَلَقَدْ زَيَّنَّا السَّمَاءَ الدُّنْيَا بِمَصَابِيحَ وَجَعَلْنَاهَا رُجُومًا لِّلشَّيَاطِينِ ۖ
وَأَعْتَدْنَا لَهُمْ عَذَابَ السَّعِيرِ ﴿٥﴾

5. And indeed, We adorned the lowest heaven with [stars like] lamps, and made them [as missiles] for stoning [eavesdropping] devils, for whom We have also prepared the torment of the Blaze.

While the previous verse mentioned how the seven skies are stacked on top of one another, this verse focuses on the beauty of the first sky by saying: **And indeed, We adorned the lowest heaven with [stars like] lamps**. The stars that light up our night-sky were made beautiful by

36 *Al-Taḥrīr wa Al-Tanwīr* 67:4, Ibn ʿĀshūr.

design. Stars are described as *maṣābīḥ*, which means 'lanterns', because they light up the night sky.[37] They are inherently bright with varying levels of light and shades, just like lanterns. Like decorations carefully placed on a mantelpiece, Allāh has adorned the world we live in with stars to make it more pleasant and attractive to the human eye. This reveals the love and care that Allāh shows towards humanity. Moreover, the beauty in this creation is a reflection of His Divine beauty, as the Prophet ﷺ would say, "Allāh is beautiful and He loves beauty."[38]

The verse also explains another function of the stars. Allāh says He has **made them [as missiles] for stoning [eavesdropping] devils**. This shows us that beyond the dimensions of the physical world, there lies a parallel spiritual world that often intersects with the physical realm.

Therefore, the stars, though millions of miles away, serve two purposes in the service of humanity. Firstly, they light up the night sky as decoration and manifestation of His beauty. Secondly, in stark contrast, they are used by Angels as weapons to frighten off devils attempting to eavesdrop into heavenly decrees that affect human lives. If such information were to be hacked by the devils, they would use it to their advantage and seek to harm people with it.

In the commentary of Imām al-Qurṭubī, he explains that the Angels harness the power of the stars to create flames (or balls of fire) from them which they hurl at the devils.[39] He explains that the stars themselves are not what is hurled towards the devils, but rather the flames taken from them. Such an understanding casts doubt upon the popular theory of shooting-stars being a manifestation of this meaning.

37 *Jāmiʿ al-Bayān fī Ta'wīl al- Qur'ān* 67:5, Imām al-Ṭabarī.
38 *Ḥadīth, Ṣaḥīḥ Muslim* 91.
39 *Al-Jāmiʿ li-Aḥkām al-Qur'ān* 67:5, by al-Qurṭubī.

According to a famous saying attributed to Qatādah, one of the foremost commentators from the third generation of Muslim scholars, "The creation of the stars is for three things: decoration of the nearest heaven, missiles to hit the devils, and signs to guide travellers."[40] Only the first two functions are mentioned in this verse.

How can the stars be used to kill devils when devils are made of fire?

To answer this question, it is necessary to understand the nature of the Jinn. Firstly, Jinn are of two types: believers and disbelievers. Disbelieving Jinn are devils who consider themselves to be the soldiers of Iblīs. It is these types of Jinn that are being spoken of in the verse. Secondly, the Qur'ān explains that all Jinn are created from a smokeless fire. However, being made from fire does not necessarily make them immune to the power of heat. Just like human beings are created from clay yet the same clay can be used to create a brick and kill a person, so too can fireballs kill the devils. In this sense, there is no contradiction in the verse of *Sūrah al-Mulk*.

Reflection

If the stars in the distant galaxies have a purpose—indeed, many purposes—how then can human beings who have been given precious life by Allāh and placed on a unique life-bearing planet think their own life is purposeless?

Also, when we read that the stars are a source of immense beauty and benefit, and at the same time a source of great pain and suffering for the devils, it allows us to appreciate how Allāh is in complete control of what benefits and what harms. He is the One who transformed the blazing fire into a cool sanctuary for Abraham, and likewise transformed the staff of Moses into a poisonous snake.

40 *Jāmiʿ al-Bayān fī Ta'wīl al-Qur'ān* 67:5, Imām al-Ṭabarī.

The lesson I take from this verse is that in life, people can experience great tragedy and yet the pain it causes can drive them into the embrace of the Almighty and motivate them to turn their life around in the most positive of ways. Therefore, let us strive to always be positive in the face of difficulties because Allāh is in control of what harms and what benefits. Perhaps the many blessings we enjoy today came about through prayers we made during tough times.

Word Bank
Section One Verses 1–5

تَبَارَكَ
Tabāraka

VERSE 1

The word tabāraka comes from same root as barakah often translated as 'blessings', but more accurately refers to the idea of something having extraordinary goodness beyond expectation.

لِيَبلُوَكُم
li-yabluwakum

VERSE 2

The word li-yabluwaku means 'to test you'. The core meaning of ibtilā revolves around the idea of testing, examining and putting to trial. The word ibtilā is the hyperbolised spelling of the word balā, thereby intensifying the meaning as if to say: a test which is thorough and ongoing.

السَّعِيرِ
Saʿīr

VERSE 5, 10, 11

The word saʿīr is translated as 'blaze', and is mentioned three times in sūrah al-Mulk. It is another name for the Hellfire and linguistically refers to a raging fire whose flames are intense.

الم

Section Two

Verses 6–12

Heaven & Hell

Section Two [Verses 6-12]

Heaven & Hell

Section two is a hard-hitting passage that lays bare the consequences of denial and disbelief in Allāh as being the Supreme Authority over the universe and beyond. It describes Hell as if it is a wild raging beast that breathes heavily as it lies in wait for its inhabitants: *They will hear it drawing in its breath when they are thrown in* (verse 7). It also describes the sense of deep regret and remorse that people who disbelieved will feel as they are hurled into the pits of the Hellfire. Here, people will confess and plead for salvation from the depths of their hearts, but to no avail. A short scene of the people of Paradise is also painted, perhaps only to further the sense of anguish felt by those destined to have no share of it.

Section Two Verses 6–12
Heaven & Hell

6. Those who disbelieve in their Lord will suffer the punishment of Hell. What an evil destination!	وَلِلَّذِينَ كَفَرُوا بِرَبِّهِمْ عَذَابُ جَهَنَّمَ ۖ وَبِئْسَ الْمَصِيرُ ﴿٦﴾
7. They will hear it drawing in its breath when they are thrown in. It blazes forth	إِذَا أُلْقُوا فِيهَا سَمِعُوا لَهَا شَهِيقًا وَهِيَ تَفُورُ ﴿٧﴾
8. Almost bursting in fury. Every time a group is cast into it, its keepers will ask them, "Did a warner not come to you?"	تَكَادُ تَمَيَّزُ مِنَ الْغَيْظِ ۖ كُلَّمَا أُلْقِيَ فِيهَا فَوْجٌ سَأَلَهُمْ خَزَنَتُهَا أَلَمْ يَأْتِكُمْ نَذِيرٌ ﴿٨﴾
9. They will say, 'Yes indeed, a warner did come to us but we denied him and said, "Allāh has sent nothing down. You are all just greatly misguided."'	قَالُوا بَلَىٰ قَدْ جَاءَنَا نَذِيرٌ فَكَذَّبْنَا وَقُلْنَا مَا نَزَّلَ اللَّهُ مِنْ شَيْءٍ إِنْ أَنْتُمْ إِلَّا فِي ضَلَالٍ كَبِيرٍ ﴿٩﴾
10. And they will lament, "If only we had listened or used our intellect, we would not be among the residents of the Blaze!"	وَقَالُوا لَوْ كُنَّا نَسْمَعُ أَوْ نَعْقِلُ مَا كُنَّا فِي أَصْحَابِ السَّعِيرِ ﴿١٠﴾
11. And so they will confess their sins. So away with the residents of the Blaze!	فَاعْتَرَفُوا بِذَنْبِهِمْ فَسُحْقًا لِأَصْحَابِ السَّعِيرِ ﴿١١﴾
12. But there is forgiveness and a great reward for those who fear their Lord though they cannot see Him.	إِنَّ الَّذِينَ يَخْشَوْنَ رَبَّهُمْ بِالْغَيْبِ لَهُمْ مَغْفِرَةٌ وَأَجْرٌ كَبِيرٌ ﴿١٢﴾

وَلِلَّذِينَ كَفَرُوا بِرَبِّهِمْ عَذَابُ جَهَنَّمَ ۖ وَبِئْسَ الْمَصِيرُ ﴿٦﴾

6. Those who disbelieve in their Lord will suffer the punishment of Hell. What an evil destination!

Just like the devils lurking in the skies above will not escape Allāh's punishment, so too will the disbelievers on the earth[41] be unable to escape it. A contrast can therefore be seen in verse 5 and 6, as if to say: the order which the Almighty maintains the heavens by empowering the Angels to harness the power of stars to use as weapons against the eavesdropping devils should serve as a reminder that He equally desires order to manifest itself here, upon the earth, if not more so. After all, Allāh has declared that human beings hold a special status before His eyes. A verse in the Qur'ān says: *Indeed, We have honoured the children of Ādam.*[42] Hence, those who disrupt such order **will suffer the punishment of Hell. What an evil destination!**

Finally, the brightly glimmering stars that decorate the night-sky, as mentioned in verse 5, are a sign for human beings to reflect over and appreciate that they too, like the stars, have a purpose in life which connects them back to their Maker.

41 *Jāmiʿ al-Bayān fī Ta'wīl al- Qur'ān* 67:5, Imām al-Ṭabarī.
42 Qur'ān 17:70.

NORMAL WORD SEQUENCE

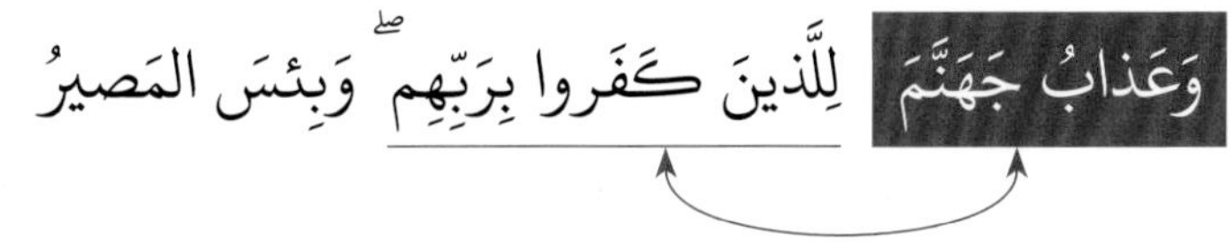

ACTUAL SEQUENCE IN THE QUR'ĀN

Qur'ānic Eloquence

The Arabic transcript of the verse has been purposefully laid out to shift greater focus onto the criminals rather than the punishment. We know this because the normal sequence of this sentence would place the words *'adhābu jahannam'* (the subject) at the beginning, whereas verse 6 places them later on (after the predicate).

This creates a rhetorical effect which shifts the reader's focus away from the subject (the punishment) and onto the predicate (the criminals),[43] as if to say: of all the crimes they could have committed they are guilty of the worst one—to disbelieve in their Lord. Moreover, the reference to God using the word *rabb,* denotes the caring, loving nature of the One who they chose to disbelieve in. Finally, by highlighting the crime of disbelief, verse 6 reminds the reader about the justice of Allāh. Punishment is only given to those guilty of committing a crime.

43 *Al-Taḥrīr wa Al-Tanwīr* 67:6, Ibn 'Āshūr.

إِذَآ أُلۡقُواْ فِيهَا سَمِعُواْ لَهَا شَهِيقًا وَهِيَ تَفُورُ ۝٧

7. They will hear it drawing in its breath when they are thrown in. It blazes forth

تَكَادُ تَمَيَّزُ مِنَ ٱلۡغَيۡظِۖ كُلَّمَآ أُلۡقِيَ فِيهَا فَوۡجٞ سَأَلَهُمۡ خَزَنَتُهَآ أَلَمۡ يَأۡتِكُمۡ نَذِيرٞ ۝٨

8. Almost bursting in fury. Every time a group is cast into it, its keepers will ask them, "Did a warner not come to you?"

Graphic scenes from the depths of Hell are now shared to intensify the warning given in verse 6. **They will hear it drawing in its breath when they are thrown in**, refers to the moment the disbelievers will be tossed into the fire of Hell[44] like lumps of wood tossed into a huge fire— a once honoured creation of God now fallen from grace due to arrogance and disbelief.

As they are about to land into the scorching fire, they **hear it drawing in its breath** (*shahīq*), where the word *shahīq* refers to a hideous, terrifying sound. This depicts Hell as a wild beast breathing heavily as it devours its prey, showing complete contempt for them.

The words **it blazes forth** translates as *tafūr*. The origin of this word *fāra* means 'to boil, flare up or burst'. It is usually used to describe water when it boils over the pan (*fawr al-mā'*).[45] This aptly captures the reaction of Hell: as it consumes the people, it furiously erupts, flames raging out of anger on behalf of the Almighty.

---

44 *Jāmiʿ al-Bayān fī Ta'wīl al- Qur'ān* 67:7, Imām al-Ṭabarī.
45 *al-Kashshāf* 67:7, al-Zamakhsharī.

The rage is so intense that the next verse says that it is **almost bursting in fury**. The word **bursting** translates as *tamayyuz* which means 'to separate out things that appear similar'.[46] This is like a scene playing out in which the dense fire of Hell erupts and expands outwards, unleashing flames into the air. Where does this rage stem from? Imām al-Biqāʿī explains that 'its rage is on behalf of its Master'[47], as if to say: it sees the disbelievers as the enemies of its Master. The Prophet ﷺ added more details to this scene when he said, 'Hell will be brought on that Day [tied down] with seventy thousand chains; and at the end of each chain will be seventy thousand angels, trying to control it.'[48]

However, the Qur'ān never mentions punishing people except that it refers to their crimes alongside it. This is why after describing the horrific nature of Hell and the torture people will face there, the verse goes on to reveal the crimes they committed.

Every time a group is cast into it, its keepers will ask them, "Did a warner not come to you?"

The word used for **group** is *fawj* which, unlike the words *ṭā'ifah, nafar, ḥizb*—all used to refer to a group elsewhere in the Qur'ān—refers to a dense crowd of people. This then reflects the sheer number of people that will be thrown into the Hellfire. Moreover, the word *kullamā,* translated here as **every time**, suggests that after one dense crowd of people has been dispatched with, another group will follow closely behind them. Yet again, the element of justice is brought to the reader's attention as when this punishment is being meted out, the Angels who are the keepers of Hell[49] will ask, **"Did a warner not come to you?"** This is a rhetorical question clarifying that such people were given ample warning and many chances to change. The illustrious Mufti of Baghdad

46 *Mufradāt Alfāẓ al-Qur'ān,* entry ميز, al-Rāghib al-Aṣfahānī.
47 *Naẓm al-Durar* 67:7, al-Biqāʿī.
48 *Ḥadīth, Ṣaḥīḥ Muslim* 2842.
49 *Al-Taḥrīr wa Al-Tanwīr* 67:8, Ibn ʿĀshūr.

during the Ottoman rule, Imām al-Ālūsī, commented on this verse saying, '[this question] inflicts a type of psychological torture which adds to their physical torture.'[50] This conveys the questioning as more of an interrogation which will create a sense of anguish for these people as they cannot dispute the fact that a warner did indeed come to them. This can all be likened to a scene from prison where the newly arrived inmates are taunted by the guards who remind them of their crimes as they lead them to their cells.

قَالُوا بَلَىٰ قَدْ جَاءَنَا نَذِيرٌ فَكَذَّبْنَا وَقُلْنَا مَا نَزَّلَ اللَّهُ مِن شَيْءٍ إِنْ أَنتُمْ إِلَّا فِي ضَلَالٍ كَبِيرٍ ٩

9. They will say, 'Yes indeed, a warner did come to us but we denied him and said, "Allāh has sent nothing down. You are all just greatly misguided."'

When the interrogation of the Day of Judgement begins, every ounce of pride and arrogance that people harbour will crumble away, and they will openly admit to their crimes and acts of disobedience. They will say: **Yes indeed, a warner did come to us but we denied him and said, "Allāh has sent nothing down..."**

As every group is about to be tossed into Hell, they will say the same thing, all expressing deep regret. However, by then, the time for confessions and change had expired. This is the underlying message such verses seek to impart, as if to say, take the opportunities of this life with both hands and use them to do good, worship God, and benefit humanity. Do this before it is too late.

50 *Rūḥ al-Maʿānī fī Tafsīr al-Qurʾān al-ʿAẓīm wa'l-Sabʿ al-Mathānī* 67:8, by al-Ālūsī.

The disbelievers, specifically, will recall the manner in which they dismissed the call of their Messengers; they would scoff at them by saying: **Allāh has sent nothing down**. They would oppose them, undermine them, and make a mockery of their message. Such behaviour would hurt the Messengers and sometimes make them even question themselves.[51] A verse in *Sūrah al-Kahf* provides insight into the type of pain the Prophet Muḥammad ﷺ would experience as a result of this. In this verse, the Almighty reassures the Prophet: *Now, perhaps you* [*O Prophet*] *will grieve yourself to death over their denial, if they* [*continue to*] *disbelieve in this message.*[52] In reality, there was never anything strange about the call of the Messengers; people were simply unwilling to let go of their lifestyles and adopt the path of faith and devotion.

The last part of the verse, **You all are just greatly misguided**, can be understood as an extension of the disbelievers' confession, or a separate comment being made by the keepers of Hell in response to the confession.

How many Messengers did each nation receive?

Interestingly, the verse ends using the plural pronoun *antum* (you all), even though each nation was typically sent only one Messenger. Why then would each group confess to calling multiple Messengers misguided? What makes this even more intriguing is that verse 9 began by speaking in the singular: **'Yes indeed, a warner did come to us,** the word warner (*nadhīr*) being singular, referring to the one Messenger that was sent to them, yet they end by saying: **You are all just greatly misguided**.

51 For instance, 12:110 in the Qur'ān: *"(Punishment was often delayed) until when the messengers were in despair and thought that they were wrong in their estimation, Our help came to them, then saved were those whom We willed. And Our punishment is not averted from the guilty."* [Translation by Mufti Taqi Usmani].

52 Qur'ān 18:6.

Firstly, it should be noted that some nations *were* sent multiple Messengers. The story of the People of the Town in *Sūrah Yāsīn* states that three Messengers were sent at the same time to one nation.[53] There is also the case of Pharaoh who was challenged by two Messengers: Mūsā and Hārūn. However, the majority of people were sent only one Messenger.

Secondly, the plural pronoun at the end reflects the fact that every nation will confess to the same crime of rejecting their Messengers in a similar manner. Therefore, even though each nation received only one Messenger, they all rejected them. Thus, **You are all just greatly misguided** can be understood as a summary of the quote of all the disbelieving nations.

Lastly, it is possible to understand that the verse distinguishes between the Messenger and his followers. In the beginning, the disbelievers admit they did indeed receive a Messenger, but they called him and his followers misguided, hence the appearance of the plural pronoun. This explanation is suggested by Shaykh Ibn ʿĀshūr.[54]

Intra-Textual Analysis

The Qur'ān is one coherent message such that passages from different parts of the Book can be compared and contrasted to extract further meaning and wisdom. For example, in verse 9 of *Sūrah al-Mulk*, the disbelievers are quoted as saying to the Messengers **Allāh has sent nothing down,** whereas the same quote, again coming from disbelievers, is mentioned in *Sūrah Yāsīn* with slightly different wording: *the Most Compassionate has sent nothing down*. The difference is very subtle:

53 Qur'ān 36:13.

54 *Al-Taḥrīr wa Al-Tanwīr* 67:9, Ibn ʿĀshūr.

REFERENCE TO GOD: ALLĀH	**REFERENCE TO GOD: AR-RAḤMĀN**
ما نَزَّلَ اللَّهُ مِن شَىءٍ	ما أَنزَلَ الرَّحمٰنُ مِن شَىءٍ
Allāh has sent nothing down	The All-Merciful has sent nothing down
SŪRAH AL-MULK	**SŪRAH YĀSĪN**

Both verses seem to be telling us what the disbelievers say to their Messengers. Why is it the case that in *Sūrah Yāsīn*, the disbelievers referred to God as *al-Raḥmān*, the Most Merciful, whereas in *Sūrah al-Mulk* they referred to Him as Allāh?

Every word-choice and turn of phrase in the Qur'ān is chosen based on Divine Wisdom, making it the most suitable and eloquent choice to fit that sentence. In this instance, the answer may lie in the fact that *Sūrah al-Mulk* is primarily a message of warning and admonition. Before this verse, many verses relating threats and punishments of destruction were delivered. For this reason, mentioning God as being Merciful would not suit the wider context. Furthermore, these are the words the disbelievers will say at a time and place where they are experiencing the pain and punishment of the Afterlife. As for the verse in *Sūrah Yāsīn*, the people who refer to God as being All-Merciful are those who think they are enjoying the blessings of God on earth; due to them having wealth and power, they think of Him as being *al-Raḥmān*.

وَقالوا لَو كُنّا نَسمَعُ أَو نَعقِلُ ما كُنّا فى أَصحابِ السَّعيرِ ﴿١٠﴾

10. And they will lament, "If only we had listened or used our intellect, we would not be among the residents of the Blaze!"

For over a hundred years, California's San Quentin State Prison has housed some of the most notorious criminals in the United States of America. It is the state's only death row for male inmates and has a gas chamber, but since 1996, the executions at the supermax prison have been carried out by lethal injection. Despite being an incredibly intimidating environment, inmates who may be serving over a hundred-year sentences manage to put on a brave face and appear unrepentant as they do their time. However, even the most hardened criminals humanity has ever seen will not be able to put on a brave face when they arrive at the gates of Hell. *Sūrah al-Mulk* informs us of their reality. A time will come when they will lament and confess: **"If only we had listened or used our intellect, we would not be among the residents of the Blaze!"**

They admit that had they listened to the warnings of the Prophet ﷺ and used their intellect, they would certainly have abandoned their immoral way of life in favour of Islam. This makes you wonder: why didn't the Quraysh of Makkah listen? Did they not hear the message of the Prophet ﷺ better than those who came in later generations?

The verse draws a distinction between hearing and listening in the context of accepting the truth. The idolaters of Makkah would have heard the advice of the Prophet ﷺ, in fact, they would have had the blessing of hearing him recite the revelation the moment it was revealed from the heavens, but they refused to pay attention, open their hearts, and listen to it. Thus, the distinction between the two is paramount—being physically able to listen does not mean you can spiritually hear the message. Indeed, a sincere person who is deaf may be affected by the message of the Prophet ﷺ more than those blessed with full hearing. Elsewhere in the Qur'ān, we learn that being made spiritually deaf is a form of punishment from Allāh: *Allāh has sealed their hearts and their hearing, and their sight is covered. They will suffer a tremendous punishment.*[55] Another verse suggests a causal link between this punishment and certain crimes the person was guilty of committing: *Woe to every sinful liar. They HEAR Allāh's revelations recited to them, then persist [in denial] arrogantly as if they did not HEAR them. So give them good news of a painful punishment.*[56]

Another reason why the verse draws our attention to the two faculties—hearing and the intellect—is because both are fundamental to establish human accountability before God.[57] When a person is unable to hear the truth or does not have a sound mind to act on it, he is not held to account for his actions. Furthermore, a person will first hear the message of the Prophet ﷺ and then their intellect will confirm its truthfulness.

55 Qur'ān 2:7.
56 Qur'ān 45:7-8.
57 *Al-Kashshāf* 67:10, al-Zamakhsharī.

However, the two could be looked at separately since the verse separates them with 'or' (*aw*): **If only we had listened or used our intellect**. This suggests that even without hearing the full message of the Prophet ﷺ, a human being can arrive at certain truths and correct moral judgements simply based on their intellect. This then redefines our understanding of what intellect is and who should be called an intelligent person. Above all else, true intelligence is when a person recognises the truth, embraces it, and acts upon it. Otherwise, a person should not be considered intelligent, even if they have a high IQ. Instead, such people will **be among the residents of the Blaze!**

The Blaze, or *saʿīr* in Arabic, is another name for Hell. Linguistically, it refers to a raging fire whose flames are intense.[58] From its origin comes the word *suʿr*, which means 'appetite' or 'hunger'.[59] The same word *suʿr* can also refer to madness or insanity.[60] Finally, the Arabs would call an iron rod used to poke a log fire a *misʿar*, from the same root as *saʿīr*, due to its effect on the fire, increasing its heat and causing the flames to rise.[61] All of these meanings could be used to further paint a graphic picture of Hell as a wild beast with an insane appetite for its inhabitants.

58 *ʿUmdat al-Ḥuffāẓ*, entry سعر, al-Samīn al-Ḥalabī.
59 *Al-Muʿjam al-Ishtiqāqī*, entry سعر, Muḥammad Ḥasan Jabal.
60 Ibid.
61 *Lane's Lexicon*, entry سعر.

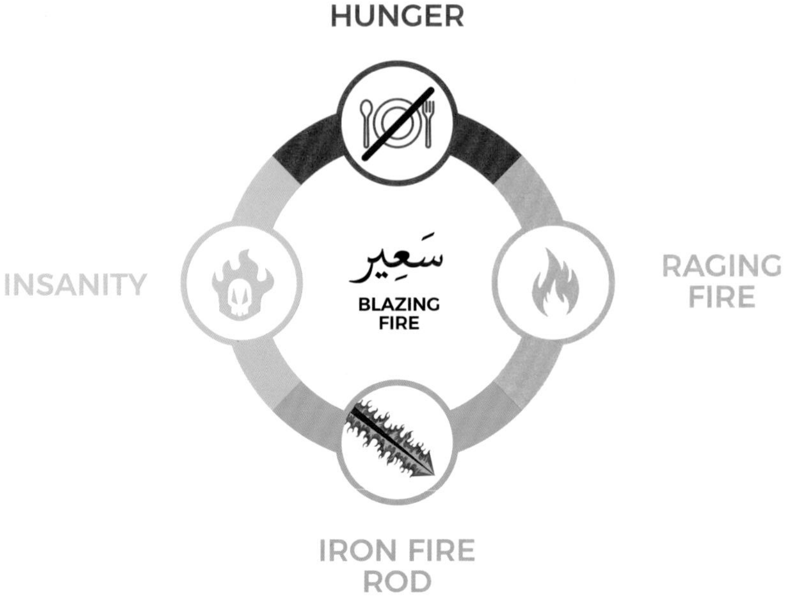

Figure 7: The four meanings of the word saʿīr 'blazing fire' in the Qur'ān

فَاعْتَرَفُوا بِذَنبِهِمْ فَسُحْقًا لِّأَصْحَابِ السَّعِيرِ ﴿١١﴾

11. And so they will confess their sins.
So away with the residents of the Blaze!

The cataclysmic events of the Final Hour, along with the horrors of the Day of Judgement, will be so overwhelming that even the most arrogant and conceited disbelievers will openly confess to their crimes.

As the saying goes: admission is the foundation to all positive change… but not in the Afterlife. In the Afterlife, confessing and admitting to past mistakes will not change the outcome of one's fate as the time for rectification was during life on this world, something already made clear earlier on in *Sūrah al-Mulk* when the Almighty said: *[He is the One] Who created death and life in order to test which of you is better in deeds.* This is why the response to their cries of guilt is simply condemnation: **So away with the residents of the Blaze!**

Interestingly, in Arabic, the central meaning of the word *iʿtarafa,* translated in this verse as 'confess', means 'to know, recognise, and acknowledge'. This highlights the fact that these people are confessing 'to committing crimes that they knew were wrong.' They felt a sense of unease and guilt in their hearts and, more importantly, that they could have done better to avoid those mistakes. This indicates self-awareness, because a person does not feel guilt for failing to do something they couldn't possibly have done any better in. For instance, if a GCSE level student was made to sit an A-level exam, he would not feel ashamed for failing to pass it. It is only when someone fails to do something they are fully capable of doing that a sense of shame and guilt arises. In fact, the feeling of guilt and anguish that one could-have and should-have done better becomes a source of psychological punishment in and of itself. The verse then tells us that this will be compounded by a physical form of punishment: **So away with the residents of the Blaze!**

Some scholars have understood **So away with the residents of the Blaze!** as a type of prayer made by God against them[62] and therefore denotes a judgement. It implies they will now be far removed from His mercy. The word *suḥq,* translated here as 'so away with', literally means to move far away to an uncharted territory, and is being used to express shock and contempt.[63]

The word 'blaze' (*saʿīr*) has now been mentioned three times in *Sūrah al-Mulk* and has been explained as referring to a raging fire with intense

62 *Al-Tashīl fī ʿUlūm al-Tanzīl* 67:12, Ibn Juzayy, 67:11, Ibn Juzayy al-Kalbī.
63 *Al-Taḥrīr wa Al-Tanwīr* 67:11, Ibn ʿĀshūr.

flames.[64] In the first instance, it was mentioned in the context of the devils (verse 5), in the second, it was in reference to humans (verse 10), and here, in its third occurrence, it combines both, referring to *saʿīr* as the home of both the devils and evil people.[65]

Allāh the Almighty does not treat anyone unfairly. In a similar verse, the disbelievers even bear witness that they deserve Hellfire, crying out, *"Yes, indeed!" But the Word of punishment has come due for the disbelievers.*[66] However, it is important to note that the door of repentance is wide open until the moment of death. As the Prophetic Narration states, "Allāh accepts a slave's repentance as long as the latter is not on his deathbed (that is, before the soul of the dying person reaches the throat.)"[67]

How many words for sin are there in the Qur'ān?

In this verse, the word used for din is *dhanb,* which is one of at least eight different words used for sin in the Qur'ān. Why is there diversity in word choice, and what make the *dhanb* type of sin different to others? A cursory look though the Qur'ān reveals that the following words all refer to acts of disobedience and sinning:

1. *Junāḥ* means to lean towards sinning or criminal activity.[68] It could refer to the intent to do something immoral, but not the act itself.[69]
2. *Ḥūb* refers to a great transgression.[70] The Qur'ān uses this word to describe the sin of people who steal from orphans[71] and hence contains the element of being an oppressive type of sin.

64 *ʿUmdat al-Ḥuffāẓ*, entry سعر, al-Samīn al-Ḥalabī.
65 *Rūḥ al-Maʿānī fī Tafsīr al-Qur'ān al-ʿAẓīm wa'l-Sabʿ al-Mathanī* 67:11, by al-Ālūsī.
66 Qur'ān 39:71.
67 *Ḥadīth*, Al-Tirmidhī 3537 [*ḥasan*].
68 *Miqyās al-Lughah*, entry ج ن ح.
69 *Muʿjam al-Furūq al-Dalāliyah,* by Muḥammad Muḥammad Dāwūd, p.34.
70 *Lisān al-ʿArab*, entry ح و ب.
71 Qur'ān 4:2 *"…nor cheat them (orphans) by mixing their wealth with your own. For this would indeed be a **great sin**."*

3. *Khaṭī'ah* literally means to miss the mark or overstep it.[72] It can be used to refer to sins that were not premeditated.
4. *Sayyi'ah* refers to sins that are vulgar[73] and as a consequence can make the appearance of the perpetrator become despicable.
5. *Fāḥishah* refers to the more indecent and shameful acts (i.e. more vulgar than the *Sayyi'ah*).[74]
6. *Munkar* is a type of act that the hearts of morally sound people feel a sense of aversion towards.
7. *Ithm* literally means to delay or neglect to do something good,[75] however in the Qur'ān, it is used to refer to the greatest of all sins: associating partners with Allāh.[76] Interestingly, the great scholar Abū Ḥayyān said, "It [*ithm*] could also [refer to an act] which the soul feels an aversion to, and the heart is not at ease with."[77]
8. Finally, we have the word *dhanb*, which is a general word that refers to both acts of indecency and self-harm.[78]

From the root of this word, we find the word *dhanab*, which means a tail, like that of a fox.[79] In Arabic literature, the tail of an animal symbolises embarrassment. It could then be said that the *dhanb* type of sins are ones that cause embarrassment and shame to the person. The word *dhanab* is also used figuratively to mean 'to follow around'[80] as a tail follows the animal. Perhaps this could deepen our understanding of the word *dhanb* as, therefore, referring to sins that haunt a person for many years later. From this perspective, we can see why Moses, when being told to return to Egypt after spending many years in exile, explained: *"but they have a claim due to sin (dhanb) against me, so I fear that they will kill me."*[81]

72 *Muʿjam al-Furūq al-Dalāliyah*, by Muḥammad Muḥammad Dāwūd, p.33.
73 *Miqyās al-Lughah*, entry س و أ.
74 *Muʿjam al-Furūq al-Dalāliyah*, by Muḥammad Muḥammad Dāwūd, p.34.
75 See *Miqyās al-Lughah*, entry أ ث م.
76 Qur'ān 4:48.
77 *Al-Baḥr al-Muḥīṭ* 2:85, Abū Ḥayyān.
78 *Muʿjam al-Furūq al-Dalāliyah*, by Muḥammad Muḥammad Dāwūd, p.41.
79 *Al-Muʿjam al-Ishtiqāqī al-Mu'aṣṣal*, entry ذنب, by Muḥammad Ḥasan Jabal.
80 Ibid.
81 Qur'ān 26:14.

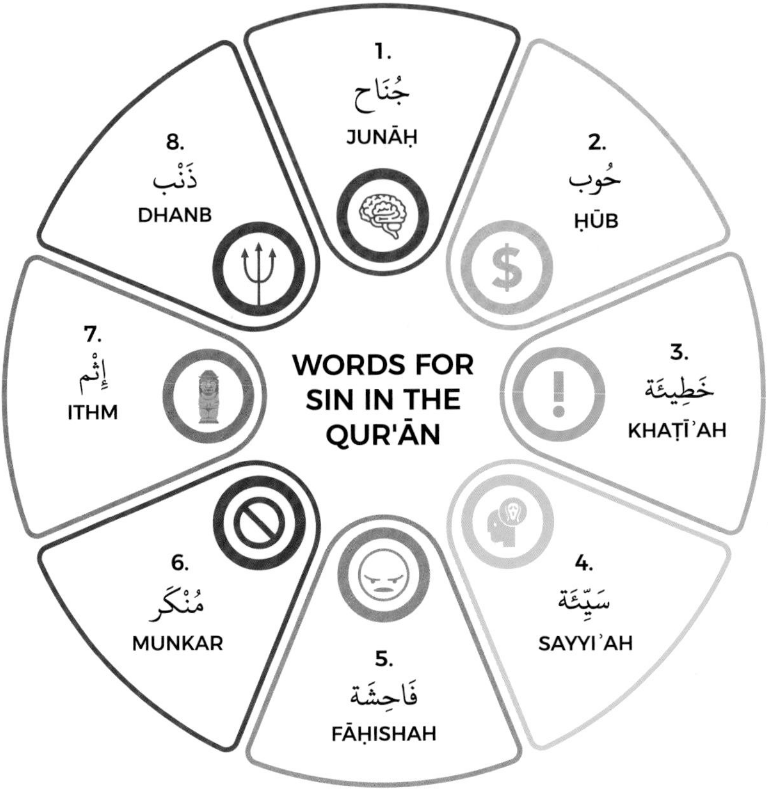

Figure 8: The 8 words for sin in the Qur'ān

إِنَّ ٱلَّذِينَ يَخۡشَوۡنَ رَبَّهُم بِٱلۡغَيۡبِ لَهُم مَّغۡفِرَةٞ وَأَجۡرٞ كَبِيرٞ ١٢

12. But there is forgiveness and a great reward for those who fear their Lord though they cannot see Him.

Unlike their disobedient counterparts, the believers will be embraced with the forgiveness of their Lord and a great reward. This strikingly sharp contrast between the believers' and disbelievers' fate as two images of the Day of Judgement placed side-by-side is a regular feature in the Qur'ān. However, in this passage, only this one verse is mentioned about the splendid fate of the believers after a number of harrowing verses warning the disbelievers of their fate. Perhaps this one verse could be seen as an extension of that warning, but from a more indirect approach, as if to say, imagine what you could have had if only you had listened and rectified yourselves: **forgiveness and a great reward**. These words themselves would be very punishing in and of themselves. What seems to strengthen this idea is the fact that the next verse returns to warning the disbelievers[82] with a more direct tone: *Whether you keep your words secret or state them openly, He knows the contents of every chest.*

Through this contrast of punishment and reward, we are given the full meaning of the statement mentioned at the outset of *Sūrah al-Mulk*: *in order to test which of you is better in deeds* (verse 2). Having already mentioned the test, the *Sūrah* completes its account by speaking of the reward for passing that test: **there is forgiveness and a great reward for those who fear their Lord though they cannot see Him**.

82 *Al-Tafsīr al-Kabīr* 67:12, al-Rāzī.

The expression: **those who fear their Lord though they cannot see Him** is translating only one of two interpretations.[83] The first being that this refers to their fear of God whom they have never seen, and the second is their fear of Him when they are alone, unseen by any human eye. Both characteristics are celebrated in the Qur'ān as they reflect purity of faith, sincerity, and feeling reverence for God. They are the hallmark of a true believer and together they qualify a person to receive what the *Sūrah* expresses in general terms as: **forgiveness and a great reward** (referring to Paradise).

The great scholar of Qur'ān, Ṭāhir b. 'Āsḥūr, commented on the sequence of the two rewards mentioned in the verse, explaining why forgiveness comes before Paradise.[84] On the Day of Judgement, the believers will be worried about the consequences of their mistakes and may continue to live with the fear that they could possibly be punished later on, even if they managed to find a place in Paradise. Therefore, by first granting them forgiveness, this sense of fear and worry is removed, allowing them to freely enjoy the rewards of Paradise to the fullest extent possible.

83 *Al-Tashīl fii 'Ulūm al-Tanzīl* 67:12, Ibn Juzayy.
84 *Al-Taḥrīr wa Al-Tanwīr* 67:12, Ibn 'Āshūr.

Reflection

Believing in the Almighty and the Afterlife without seeing it shows how intellectually discerning the believers are. Unlike the disbelievers who confessed: *If only we had listened or used our intellect* (verse 10), believers understand that faith in God is a rational conclusion even though one cannot see Him. They reflect over the signs in nature and within their own selves; they take heed of the warnings in revelation and contemplate deeply on what the Prophet ﷺ has advised them. For this reason, they qualify for the great reward of Paradise. The real test of a person in this world is to use their intellect and reasoning to seek the truth and follow what the Almighty has revealed through His prophets of truth. He who succeeds in this test deserves every reward of God, and he who fails in it is not an intelligent person, even though he might be known as a great philosopher or scientist.

Word Bank
Section Two Verses 6–12

VERSE 8

فَوجٌ
Fawj

The word fawj is translated as 'group', unlike the words ṭā'ifah, nafar, ḥizb - all used with the meaning of 'group' elsewhere in the Qur'ān- fawj refers to a dense crowd of people.

VERSE 11

اعْتَرَفَ
I'tarafa

The central meaning of the word i'tarafa, translated in verse 9 as 'confess', means 'to know, recognise, and acknowledge'.

VERSE 11

ذَنْب
Dhanb

From the root of this word we find the word dhanab which means a tail, like the tail of a fox. In Arabic literature the tail of animal symbolises embarrassment. Based on this dhanb refers to sins that cause embarrassment and bring shame.

الملك

Section Three

Verses 13–22

Danger is imminent unless you change

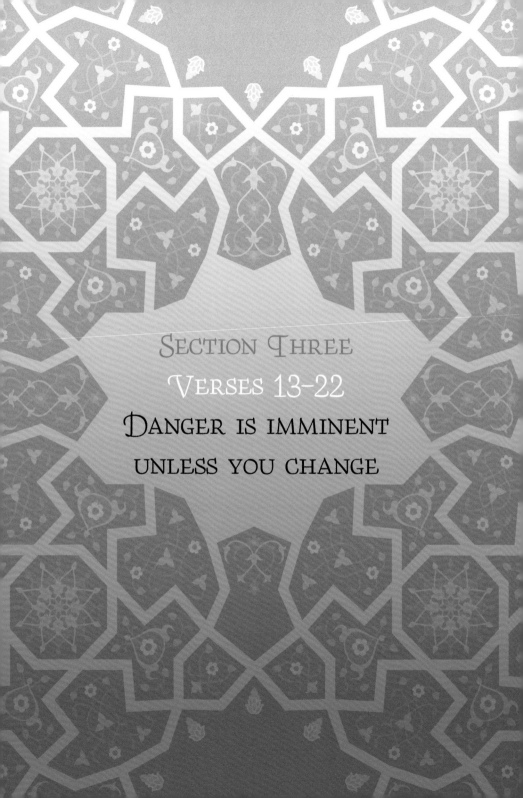

Section Three [Verses 13–22]

Danger is imminent unless you change

Section three addresses the stubbornness of people and their unwillingness to let go of their false beliefs. It contains verses that confront those who feel a false sense of safety and security on earth, awakening them to what the power of Allāh's Will may bring about. Threats are issued of the earth quaking beneath their feet to swallow them up. The *Sūrah* then shakes them even harder so that they realise that nothing can withstand Allāh's Power, which they hardly ever take into account: "*Is this your [pathetic] army who will aid you against the Lord of Mercy? Indeed, the disbelievers are only [lost] in delusion!*" (Verse 20). It then calls upon them to reflect on the flight of birds, a sign in nature and an aspect of creation they see frequently but rarely contemplate the spiritual significance of. However, this is simply a moment of quiet before another storm of threats and warnings: "*Who can provide for you if He withholds His provision? Yet they persist in their arrogance and aversion [to the truth]*" (Verse 21). Section three ends by painting a vivid picture of such people, showing the decrepit nature of their condition compared to those who are humble enough to submit their will to Allāh: "*Now, who is better guided: the one who crawls facedown or the one who walks upright on the Straight Path?*" (Verse 22)

Section Three Verses 13–22
Danger is imminent unless you change

13. Whether you keep your words secret or state them openly, He knows the contents of every chest.	وَأَسِرُّوا قَوۡلَكُمۡ أَوِ اجۡهَرُوا بِهِۦٓۖ إِنَّهُۥ عَلِيمُۢ بِذَاتِ الصُّدُورِ ١٣
14. How could He who created not know, when He is the Most Subtle, the All-Aware?	أَلَا يَعۡلَمُ مَنۡ خَلَقَ وَهُوَ اللَّطِيفُ الۡخَبِيرُ ١٤
15. He is the One Who smoothed out the earth for you, so move about in its regions and eat from His provisions. And to Him is the resurrection [of all].	هُوَ ٱلَّذِي جَعَلَ لَكُمُ ٱلۡأَرۡضَ ذَلُولٗا فَٱمۡشُواْ فِي مَنَاكِبِهَا وَكُلُواْ مِن رِّزۡقِهِۦۖ وَإِلَيۡهِ ٱلنُّشُورُ ١٥
16. Do you feel secure that the One Who is in heaven will not cause the earth to swallow you up as it quakes violently?	ءَأَمِنتُم مَّن فِي ٱلسَّمَآءِ أَن يَخۡسِفَ بِكُمُ ٱلۡأَرۡضَ فَإِذَا هِيَ تَمُورُ ١٦
17. Or do you feel secure that the One Who is in heaven will not unleash upon you a storm of stones. Only then would you know how [serious] My warning was!	أَمۡ أَمِنتُم مَّن فِي ٱلسَّمَآءِ أَن يُرۡسِلَ عَلَيۡكُمۡ حَاصِبٗاۖ فَسَتَعۡلَمُونَ كَيۡفَ نَذِيرِ ١٧

18. And certainly those before them denied [as well], then how severe was My response!	وَلَقَدْ كَذَّبَ ٱلَّذِينَ مِن قَبْلِهِمْ فَكَيْفَ كَانَ نَكِيرِ ﴿١٨﴾
19. Have they not seen the birds above them, spreading and closing their wings? It is only the Lord of Mercy who holds them up. Indeed, He is All-Seeing of everything.	أَوَلَمْ يَرَوْا۟ إِلَى ٱلطَّيْرِ فَوْقَهُمْ صَٰٓفَّٰتٍ وَيَقْبِضْنَ ۚ مَا يُمْسِكُهُنَّ إِلَّا ٱلرَّحْمَٰنُ ۚ إِنَّهُۥ بِكُلِّ شَىْءٍۭ بَصِيرٌ ﴿١٩﴾
20. Is this your [pathetic] army who will aid you against the Lord of Mercy? Indeed, the disbelievers are only [lost] in delusion!	أَمَّنْ هَٰذَا ٱلَّذِى هُوَ جُندٌ لَّكُمْ يَنصُرُكُم مِّن دُونِ ٱلرَّحْمَٰنِ ۚ إِنِ ٱلْكَٰفِرُونَ إِلَّا فِى غُرُورٍ ﴿٢٠﴾
21. Who can provide for you if He withholds His provision? Yet they persist in their arrogance and aversion [to the truth].	أَمَّنْ هَٰذَا ٱلَّذِى يَرْزُقُكُمْ إِنْ أَمْسَكَ رِزْقَهُۥ ۚ بَل لَّجُّوا۟ فِى عُتُوٍّ وَنُفُورٍ ﴿٢١﴾
22. Now, who is better guided: the one who crawls facedown or the one who walks upright on the Straight Path?	أَفَمَن يَمْشِى مُكِبًّا عَلَىٰ وَجْهِهِۦٓ أَهْدَىٰٓ أَمَّن يَمْشِى سَوِيًّا عَلَىٰ صِرَٰطٍ مُّسْتَقِيمٍ ﴿٢٢﴾

وَأَسِرُّوا قَوْلَكُمْ أَوِ اجْهَرُوا بِهِ ۖ إِنَّهُ عَلِيمٌ بِذَاتِ الصُّدُورِ ﴿١٣﴾

13. Whether you keep your words secret or state them openly, He knows the contents of every chest.

The *Sūrah* now turns its attention back on the disbelievers, as if to say: whether you try to hide your real motives or speak of them publicly in defiance, it is all the same because Allāh's knowledge is perfect and, therefore, nothing is hidden from Him.[85] It can also be read as an explanation of the previous verse, underlining the reason why some people *fear their Lord though they cannot see Him*—it is precisely because they were convinced that **whether you keep your words secret or state them openly, He knows the contents of every chest**. When a person truly internalises this in their heart, they would feel embarrassed to even think of committing sins.

Reflection

In life, you come across people who are really good at reading others. They can guess what's on your mind and can even complete your sentences for you. However, sometimes one can become confused and unable to figure out what's going on in your own head until you sit and talk to someone about what's on your mind. This verse is teaching us that when those thoughts or feelings first began to pass through your head, Allāh knew of it in better detail than you came to know after all that discussion and introspection. Ultimately, the verse is a wake-up call to be honest and genuine with Allāh and the people in your life. Being aware of the extent of Allāh's knowledge can help correct the insincerity within your heart. When a person becomes more sincere, he will worship Allāh more often with greater humility and devotion. In a reassuring Prophetic Narration, we read, *"Allāh has accepted my invocation (duʿā')*

85 *Jāmiʿ al-Bayān fī Ta'wīl al- Qur'ān* 67:13, Imām al-Ṭabarī.

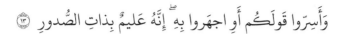

to forgive the passing thoughts that occur in the hearts of my followers, unless they put it to action or utter it."[86]

The verse logically concludes itself by saying that Allāh **knows 'the content of the chest**,' which implies that anything greater than a thought or feeling must, therefore, also be known. The word *ʿAlīm* is mentioned, which is the more intense spelling of the name *ʿĀlim*, both of which mean 'All Knower'. However, *ʿAlīm* carries a more emphatic and powerful meaning.[87] In the 50th chapter of the Qur'ān, a greater insight is given into the scale of Allāh's knowledge: *Indeed, [it is] We [Who] created humankind and [fully] know what their souls whisper to them, and We are closer to them than [their] jugular vein.*[88] This is why secrets or confessions are all the same to the Almighty. Some scholars went as far as to analyse why Allāh said He knows the secret and open words, instead of phrasing it is knowing the open and secret words. Analysing this, Imām al-Ālūsī states:"Secrets were mentioned before openly spoken words to show that they have been exposed and that what they had always feared (exposure) has now occurred. It is also a type of hyperbole to indicate Allāh's comprehensive knowledge, one that is all-encompassing of all that can be known, almost as though His knowledge of what they conceal is more than His knowledge of what they publicise, though of course in reality there is no difference."[89]

أَلَا يَعْلَمُ مَنْ خَلَقَ وَهُوَ اللَّطِيفُ الْخَبِيرُ ﴿١٤﴾

14. How could He who created not know, when He is the Most Subtle, the All-Aware?

86 *Ḥadīth, Ṣaḥīḥ al-Bukhārī* 5269.
87 *Al-Taḥrīr wa Al-Tanwīr* 67:13, Ibn ʿĀshūr.
88 Qur'ān 50:16.
89 *Rūḥ al-Maʿānī fī Tafsīr al-Qur'ān al-ʿAẓīm wa'l-Sabʿ al-Mathānī* 67:2, by al-Ālūsī.

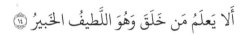

This statement makes it clear as to the reason why the Almighty is aware of every hidden and apparent issue as stated in the previous verse: *Whether you keep your words secret or state them openly, He knows the contents of every chest.* In fact, this challenges any who doubt the idea of God knowing what is in their hearts with a compelling rational argument, and that is to say: the designer and manufacturer of an item will automatically know the most about the product. What then if the product is only able to operate by the power and will of its Maker? Reflecting upon this is truly awe-inspiring.

It is ludicrous for anyone to think something can be hidden from Allāh when their minds in which they try to hide their intentions were created by Him and He knows all its pathways and hidden corners. Indeed, the intentions they seek to hide are also part of Allāh's creation; He knows how they formulate and where they lodge. How can He who created all the systems within the cosmos, and by whose command the whole machinery of this universe is functioning, be unaware of any part of it? A closer look at the Arabic wording of the verse reveals a broader meaning beyond Allāh knowing just the thoughts and intentions of people.[90] This is because the verse does not explicitly say, "How could He who created not know *the thoughts or secrets of people?*" Instead, it is left open: **How could He who created not know...** The implication of this being that His knowledge captures those thoughts and much more beside them— since everything in existence has been created by Him, He automatically knows everything about everything.

Another interpretation of the phrase is that the Arabic word *man* is the direct object i.e. "Does He not know *who* He created?"

90 Al-Biqāʿī.

In any case, the core meaning of this verse resonates with the overarching message of *Sūrah al-Mulk* which revolves around the power and control of Allāh over the universe, as knowledge is a form of power. For instance, one way a threat can be made is when a person, let us say someone who until this point was a complete stranger, asks you to hand over your belongings in a dark alley without any show of force. Naturally, you refuse, but then they start relating information about your private life and hinting at details concerning your spouse and children. No threat has been made, yet this man has knowledge, which translates into leverage and power. This is how knowledge equates to power. If Allāh knows everything, as this verse suggests, then how much power should we attribute to Him?

The verse ends: **when He is the Most Subtle, the All-Aware?** which serves to increase the strength of the argument; as if to say, not only does He know about His creation on account of Him being their Maker, but He is also the Most Subtle (*laṭīf*) and All-Aware (*khabīr*). The great scholar, Ibn ʿĀshūr, says these two Names not only underscore the message of the previous verse about Allāh knowing people's secrets, but also goes further to broaden it by alluding to the fact that He knows even more hidden matters than the secrets that people keep.[91]

Two Beautiful Names of Allāh: *al-Laṭīf* and *al-Khabīr*

There are many names that refer to Allāh's knowledge and its all-encompassing nature. He is the All-Knowing, *al-ʿAlīm*, who knows things in the most complete and perfect manner; He is the Wise, *al-Ḥakīm*, who knows how to perfectly apply His knowledge with wisdom. He is the Witness, *al-Shahīḍ*, who possesses an eye-witness account of things; the Preserver, *al-Ḥafīẓ*, and the Enumerator, *al-Muḥṣī*, who knows the quantities of things and comprehends all.

---

91 *Al-Taḥrīr wa Al-Tanwīr* 67:14, Ibn ʿĀshūr.

As for the two names mentioned in verse 14, *al-Laṭīf* and *al-Khabīr*, then *al-Laṭīf* can be translated as The Subtle One or The Most Discerning. According to Imām al-Rāzī, the first meaning intended in this verse is the second name, *al-Khabīr*, which also relates to the idea of Allāh being discerning and knowing the intricacies of all things.[92] Shaykh Ibn ʿĀshūr says that the meaning of *al-Laṭīf* also includes the idea of Allāh managing the affairs of the world with care and wisdom.[93]

Reflection

Allāh is extremely subtle and caring in how He brings about change in our lives and creates transformation in the world. The path of change is often long and drawn out. Consider the rise of young Yūsuf to the throne of Egypt from where it all began at the bottom of a hopeless well. It was the Almighty who shaped that path to victory for him, paving it out with many twists and turns. No one could have predicted his life's trajectory. The Qur'ān tells us that after being reunited with his family and whilst looking back at his turbulent life, Yūsuf says, with an almost newfound appreciation of who Allāh is: *"Indeed my Lord is subtle (laṭīf) in fulfilling what He wills. Surely, He [alone] is the All-Knowing, All-Wise."*[94] His life experience taught him that Allāh is *Laṭīf*. Appreciating this attribute of Allāh can become a huge source of positivity for a person facing adversity and hardship.

Interestingly, the name *al-Laṭīf* occurs seven times in the Qur'ān, five of which are coupled with the name *al-Khabīr*. The pairing of these Names reveals even more insight and wisdom. It is like Allāh is telling us that He plans out the events of the world in a very subtle but caring manner and that planning and governing is done based on expert knowledge of both the hidden and apparent. When we plan in life, we do so oftentimes

92 *Al-Tafsīr al-Kabīr* 67:14, al-Rāzī.
93 *Al-Taḥrīr wa Al-Tanwīr* 67:14, Ibn ʿĀshūr.
94 Qur'ān 12:100.

without proper consideration for all the factors at play, however since Allāh plans out our lives, and because He is *al-Khabīr*, all the factors that need to be considered are incorporated into that plan. Knowing this should help us trust more in His plan than our own.

هُوَ ٱلَّذِى جَعَلَ لَكُمُ ٱلْأَرْضَ ذَلُولًا فَٱمْشُوا۟ فِى مَنَاكِبِهَا وَكُلُوا۟ مِن
رِّزْقِهِۦ ۖ وَإِلَيْهِ ٱلنُّشُورُ ﴿١٥﴾

15. He is the One Who smoothed out the earth for you, so move about in its regions and eat from His provisions. And to Him is the resurrection [of all].

Amongst the countless favours that Allāh has blessed humanity with is that He **smoothed out the earth for you**. Though human beings have inhabited this earth for over a hundred thousand years, how many have recognised this as a divine blessing and thanked the Almighty?

The words **smoothed out** is a translation of the Arabic word *dhalūl*, which is normally used to describe an animal that has been tamed so that a human can use it as a mount or for labour. Its core-meaning (*dhull*) revolves around the idea of subjugation and being humbled. This word is used in this verse to describe the earth's nature as one by which people can use it to serve their own interests, despite it being greater in size and much tougher than them.[95] It is as if a likeness is being struck of the earth being similar to a wild animal, that had it not been tamed and made humble by Allāh, human beings would be unable to survive on it.

95 *Al-Taḥrīr wa Al-Tanwīr* 67:15, Ibn ʿĀshūr.

Cueva de las Manos, Perito Moreno, Argentina. The human hand artwork in the cave is dated between 13,000–9,000 BC.

Reflection

Modern-day science has allowed us to appreciate this meaning from yet another perspective. The earth is revolving at a speed of 1,000 miles per hour and, at the same time, moves in its orbit around the sun at a speed of approximately 65,000 miles per hour. Furthermore, the earth, the sun, and the solar system travel in space at a speed of around 20,000 miles per hour. Despite such speedy movements, people walk on its surface with such stability that they are oblivious to such realities, when meanwhile, the earth is gliding along its axis at a fixed angle of 23.5 degrees.

The experts in Qur'ānic commentary explain the details of this idea of the earth being 'smoothed out' in a number of ways:

1. The ground beneath our feet is made of soft soil such that it can be dug up to place the foundations of our homes, find fresh water, and mine for useful resources such as oil and gas.
2. The earth has been stabilised with mountains that prevent it from falling out of orbit.[96] As mentioned elsewhere in the Qur'ān: *'He placed firm mountains on the earth—in case it should shake under you.'*[97]
3. Allāh did not make the surface of the earth rough and irregular. For the most part, it is not a jagged mountainous terrain but smooth, flat, and easily traversable.[98]
4. Allāh did not make the ground out of hard metal like iron as this would create unbearable heat conditions during the summer and extreme cold during the winter. Moreover, it would make farming and agriculture impossible.[99]

96 *Al-Jāmiʿ li-Aḥkām al-Qur'ān* 67:15, by al-Qurṭubī.
97 Qur'ān 31:10.
98 *Al-Tafsīr al-Kabīr* 67:15, al-Rāzī.
99 Ibid.

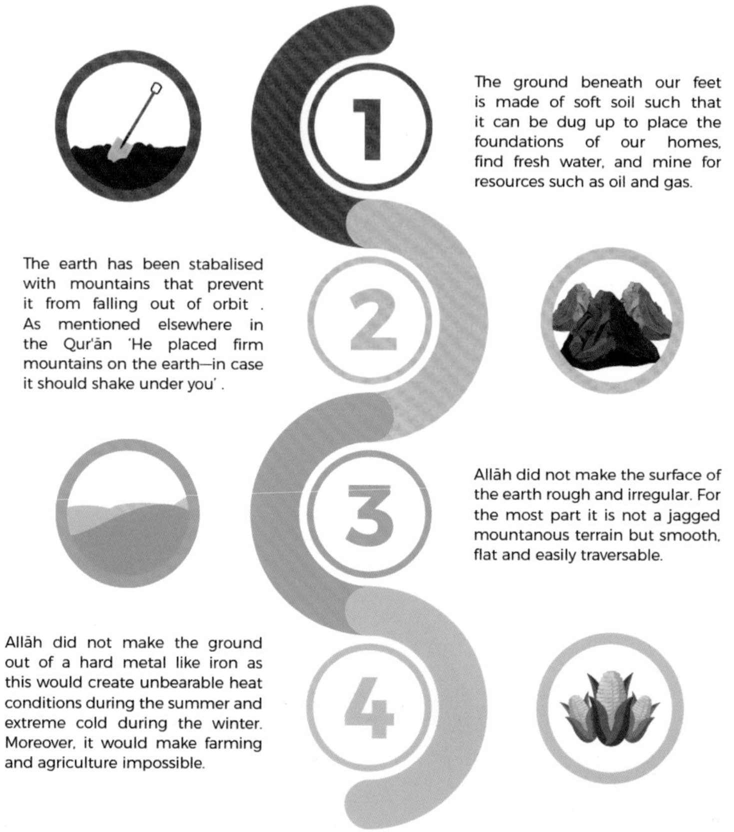
1
The ground beneath our feet is made of soft soil such that it can be dug up to place the foundations of our homes, find fresh water, and mine for resources such as oil and gas.
2
The earth has been stabalised with mountains that prevent it from falling out of orbit . As mentioned elsewhere in the Qur'ān 'He placed firm mountains on the earth—in case it should shake under you' .
3
Allāh did not make the surface of the earth rough and irregular. For the most part it is not a jagged mountanous terrain but smooth, flat and easily traversable.
4
Allāh did not make the ground out of a hard metal like iron as this would create unbearable heat conditions during the summer and extreme cold during the winter. Moreover, it would make farming and agriculture impossible.

Figure 9: The 4 meanings of the phrase "He smoothed out the earth for you"

This verse places these blessings before humanity's eyes using a turn of phrase that everyone, regardless of whether they live in the concrete jungle or out in the countryside, can appreciate.

The third view regarding the earth being smoothed out such that traversing it has been made easy for people lends itself well to the meaning of the second part of the verse: **so move about in its regions and eat from His provisions**. The two parts are thus wonderfully linked as Allāh first informs us that He made the earth smooth and flat as if it is humbling itself to humans, and then He tells us to travel and explore its **regions** (*manākib*), referring to the furthest most remote areas. The ability to travel to such places, even the most remote parts of the world, is proof that He has smoothed it out for humanity (i.e. made it *dhalūl*). In fact, the words **and eat from His provisions** suggest that people will be able to find resources and riches in even the most remote parts of the world or places of extreme weather conditions like the Eskimos do.

Machu Picchu, Peru: a 15th-century Inca citadel, located in southern Peru, built on a 7,970 ft mountain ridge

The verse ends: **And to Him is the resurrection [of all]**, where the word 'resurrection' is translating *nushūr.* The root meaning of this word means to spread out, unfold, or to scatter.[100] It is classically used to refer to the spreading out of sheep as they are released from their night-time enclosure. In the context of this verse, it refers to how mankind will emerge from their graves on the Day of Judgement and spread out aimlessly, in every direction, out of terror and fright. As the Almighty says elsewhere in the Qur'ān: *'With eyes downcast, they will come forth from the graves as if they were swarming locusts.'*[101]

ءَأَمِنتُم مَّن فِي ٱلسَّمَآءِ أَن يَخۡسِفَ بِكُمُ ٱلۡأَرۡضَ فَإِذَا هِيَ تَمُورُ
أَمۡ أَمِنتُم مَّن فِي ٱلسَّمَآءِ أَن يُرۡسِلَ عَلَيۡكُمۡ حَاصِبٗاۖ
فَسَتَعۡلَمُونَ كَيۡفَ نَذِيرِ
وَلَقَدۡ كَذَّبَ ٱلَّذِينَ مِن قَبۡلِهِمۡ فَكَيۡفَ كَانَ نَكِيرِ ١٦-١٨

16-18. Do you feel secure that the One Who is in heaven will not cause the earth to swallow you up as it quakes violently? Or do you feel secure that the One Who is in heaven will not unleash upon you a storm of stones. Only then would you know how [serious] My warning was! And certainly those before them denied [as well], then how severe was My response!

Whereas the previous verse employed gentle reasoning and encouraged reflection over nature to arrive at the truth, verse 16 and 17 warns people who have long felt secure in their life on earth that events such as earthquakes, tornados and hurricanes can easily be unleashed upon them as a form of worldly punishment for ungratefulness towards their Maker: **Do you feel secure that the One Who is in heaven will not cause the earth to swallow you up as it quakes violently?**

---

100 *Lane's Lexicon*, entry ن ش ر.
101 Qur'ān 54:7.

The people living on earth benefiting from the way it has been smoothed out and yet fail to worship the giver of this gift need to realize that this blessing could easily be reversed and turned into a curse, bringing with it suffering and devastation. This is in stark contrast to what the previous verse said. Verse 15 refers to the earth as being *dhalūl*, i.e. humbled, whereas this verse states that the same earth could easily **swallow you up**. This daunting meaning is made more powerful with the use of the phrase: **as it quakes violently**, as if to say, Allāh will cause the earth to simultaneously quake and shake whilst they are being swallowed up by it.[102] A similar message is echoed elsewhere in the Qur'ān: '*Say, "He [alone] has the power to unleash upon you a torment from above or below you or split you into [conflicting] factions and make you taste the violence of one another." See how We vary the signs, so perhaps they will comprehend.*'[103]

Reflection

This verse highlights the complete control Allāh the Almighty has over His creation, something further magnified by the fact that He is **the One Who is in heaven**, and yet from such a far-away place is able to control the ground beneath our feet. It also teaches us the importance of showing gratitude to Allāh by using the resources He has placed on this planet responsibly and adopting policies that allow for them to regenerate sustainably.

The next verse strikes another blow against the stubborn-hearted: **Or do you feel secure that the One Who is in heaven will not unleash upon you a storm of stones. Only then would you know how [serious] My warning was!**

While the previous verse warned of a punishment that would come from beneath man's feet, this verse warns of a punishment that will

102 *Al-Tafsīr al-Kabīr* 67:16, al-Rāzī.
103 Qur'ān 6:65.

be unleashed from above. However, both begin with the rhetorical question: **do you feel secure**, highlighting the degree of complacency that has set within some people's hearts, such that they trivialise the consequences of disobeying their Maker.

There are two possible explanations as to what type of punishment this verse is referring to, depending on how the word *ḥāṣiban* is interpreted. Imām Ibn Juzayy said it can refer to either a hail of stones raining down or a violent destructive wind,[104] such as a tornado.

Perhaps the selection of punishment carries a deeper meaning that would resonate with the idolaters of Makkah, for they secured their high status of being divinely protected ever since Abraha, the Abyssinian general, and his army were destroyed by a hail of stones from the sky when they tried to attack the Kaʿbah in the year the Prophet ﷺ was born. With this in mind, the deeper meaning, would be for the polytheists to reflect over their situation as they were now taking the place of Abraha and became liable for the same punishment due to preventing the Prophet ﷺ from liberating the Kaʿbah of idolatry.

Why punish from the ground and then the sky?

The earth is described in very affectionate terms throughout the Qur'ān. It is described as being like a resting place[105] (*mihād*), like a carpet[106] (*firāsh*), like a living quarter (*mustaqar*),[107] and as being submissive to people (*dhalūl*).[108] Piecing this together, we see another expression of God's mercy, in which the earth is serving humanity out of submission to its Maker.

104 *Al-Tashīl li-ʿUlūm al-Tanzīl*, 67:17, Ibn Juzayy al-Kalbī.
105 Qur'ān 78:6.
106 Qur'ān 2:22.
107 Qur'ān 7:24.
108 Qur'ān 67:15.

In a similar way, the sky has also been described as being in the service of humanity. The Qur'ān says it is a canopy[109] (*binā'*) that has been decorated with lanterns[110] (*maṣābīḥ*) by the Almighty for our enjoyment. It contains stars whose fire is used by angels to create weapons to use against devils trying to interfere in the world of humans, and yet the same stars are stationed precisely to allow the traveller to use them as a guide, like a map placed in the sky.

Of the two—the earth and sky—the closest is the earth, and in the domain of evil, it is abused far more than the sky. This is perhaps one reason for it being mentioned first. Additionally, a stubborn person hearing these verses may take the threat of the quaking ground and think they could escape to a nearby hill or mountain, but then they are told about a punishment unleashed from the sky raining down upon them, thereby creating an all-encompassing threatening scenario.

The last verse (18) from this passage concludes with a stark reminder: **And certainly those before them denied [as well], then how severe was My response!**[111] Whereas the previous two verses contained threats relating to the future, this verse instructs the disbelievers to look at the history of perished nations. If they consider these as empty threats, they need only look at the great nations before them, now utterly destroyed.

The verse also transitions away from the second person narrative (**do you feel secure**) to the third person (**certainly those before them**) in order to express Allāh's contempt with them, as if to say He is done with them and does not want to speak to them anymore.

109 Qur'ān 2:22.
110 Qur'ān 67:5.
111 'My Response' is the translation of the Arabic word *nakīr*.

Reflection

The Qur'ān will often relate historical accounts of previous nations that perished despite their great material achievements. The lesson we can draw from such accounts is that Allāh has a universal law or policy that will never be changed or bypassed. Those who belie the message will surely receive punishment. It does not matter how well-off you are or how technologically advanced the people may be, we should not consider ourselves an exception to this rule. On a more personal level, as Muslims we should not reject, deny, or even hold reservations about any Islamic teaching or instruction. If you don't understand something from Islam—and yet you know for sure it is from Islam— tell yourself there is a wisdom which you are not yet seeing due to a lack of knowledge on your part. Once a person learns more about this beautiful religion, the stronger their convictions will grow, and soon enough the doubts will topple one after another.

أَوَلَمْ يَرَوْا۟ إِلَى ٱلطَّيْرِ فَوْقَهُمْ صَـٰٓفَّـٰتٍ وَيَقْبِضْنَ ۚ مَا يُمْسِكُهُنَّ إِلَّا ٱلرَّحْمَـٰنُ ۚ
إِنَّهُۥ بِكُلِّ شَىْءٍۭ بَصِيرٌ ﴿١٩﴾

19. Have they not seen the birds above them, spreading and closing their wings? It is only the Lord of Mercy who holds them up. Indeed, He is All-Seeing of everything.

The strong warnings of the previous verses now give way to a gentle invitation to reflect: **Have they not seen the birds above them, spreading and closing their wings?**

The flight of birds is an aspect of creation people see frequently but rarely do they marvel over its beauty and draw spiritual signs from it. Watching a bird gliding is truly a thing of magnificence. It seems almost stationary, suspended in mid-air as if by magic. With outstretched wings, feathers in perfect alignment, a bird in flight is an image of peace, serenity, and grace. Does an object suspending itself in mid-air not defy logic? Who gave these creatures such an extraordinary ability to the exception of others? Doesn't the one responsible for this deserve praise and glorification?

In particular, this verse highlights the mechanics involved in the flight of birds through two keywords: *ṣāffāt* and *yaqbiḍn,* translated here as 'spreading' and 'closing'. The first word *ṣāffāt* literally means 'rows', which refers to the wings being outstretched when the bird is drifting in the sky mid-flight. This links to the root meaning of 'rows', for when the wings are spread out, they form a straight horizontal line.[112] The second word, *yaqbiḍn,* refers to the beating of wings which birds manage by using their strong breast muscles in order to take flight, obtain thrust, or make a landing. The word literally means to 'take a hold of', referring to the wings as they are folded up like a tightening grip.

A closer examination of the Arabic word reveals a subtle difference in the word choice; the word selected for 'closing' (*yaqbiḍn*) is a present-tense verb, whereas the word for 'spreading' (*ṣāffāt*) is a noun. The difference is that a present-tense verb can carry the meaning of repetition or something being momentary, as oppose to permanent, which is what a noun expresses. This verb-noun differentiation captures the nuances of the flight mechanics as the bird needs to flap and beat its wings repeatedly for a short moment to take flight, whereas the noun is used to refer to the idea of 'spreading' as once it has taken off, it can stay gliding in the air for long periods of time through the shape created by the outstretched wings. Furthermore, of the two states, spreading open the wings is the default, whereas beating is the exception.

Contrary to what some people claim, this phenomenon is not the product of an undirected random sequence of gene mutations acted on by natural selection. The verse underlines this point when it says: **It is only the Lord of Mercy who holds them up**. Not only is it the case

112 *Al-Taḥrīr wa Al-Tanwīr* 67:19, Ibn 'Āshūr.

that birds were fashioned to facilitate flight through the design of their wing structures and feathers, but also the air in the sky was created in a way that allows for the flight of birds and planes. This is much like the water in the ocean and how it was designed to carry ships. The main idea is to see the world around us through the lens of spirituality and god-consciousness. Only those blessed with faith will look to nature and see such signs living around them, calling them to a deeper connection with Allāh.

Intra-*Sūrah* Connections

Imām al-Qurṭubī suggests that this verse is linked to verse 15, in which Allāh declared that He was responsible for making the earth submissive for humans, as this verse declares that Allāh has also made the air submissive to birds, such that they can use it to facilitate their travel, migration, and hunting, just like we can use the earth for travel and business.[113]

Earlier in verse 3, Allāh told people to look up at something else more distant which also contains signs, alluding to the power of the Almighty: *[He is the One] Who created seven heavens, one above the other. You will never see any imperfection in the creation of the Most Compassionate. So look again: do you see any flaws?* The difference is that here, in verse 20, the place of reflection is closer to the human eye, for the birds are nearer and more visible than the stars. In this way, *Sūrah al-Mulk* intensifies its call for people to be more reflective and draw upon their spiritual intelligence.

113 *Al-Jāmiʿ li-Aḥkām al-Qur'ān* 67:19, by al-Qurṭubī.

Reflection

Interestingly, the word 'power' of Allāh is not referred to in the verse but rather 'The All Merciful'. It is the mercy, love, and care of Allāh that created the phenomena of flight and everything good that comes from that, such as the beauty in nature in seeing birds decorating the sky, the pollination of trees by insects and birds, the luxury of air-travel, and so on. Everything hinges on the mercy of Allāh, such that its absence would lead to the collapse of the entire system. This should inspire us to be grateful and thankful to Allāh.

The verse ends by highlighting the fact that Allāh sees everything: **Indeed, He is All-Seeing of everything**. Why is the attribute of God's sight drawn to our attention here?

Firstly, the verse begins with the rhetorical question: 'Do they not see?' So Allāh sees all and these people failing to recognise even the most basic of realities.

Secondly, as mentioned by Imām al-Zamakhsharī,[114] this last phrase can be interpreted to mean: 'He knows how He creates and how He puts such wonders into motion'. This suggests the attribute of 'seeing' *(baṣīrah)* is also related to seeing in a figurative sense, i.e. to have insight into something. About this, Imām al-Ṭabarī[115] said, 'Allāh possesses complete insight into everything and has detailed knowledge of everything. There is no inconsistency in His command, and nor can any *tafāwut* be seen in His creation' — where *tafāwut* was mentioned in the verse before and means 'discrepancy' and 'imbalance'.

114 *Al-Kashshāf* 67:19, al-Zamakhsharī.
115 *Jāmiʿ al-Bayān fī Ta'wīl al-Qur'ān* 67:19, Imām al-Ṭabarī.

أَمَّنْ هَٰذَا ٱلَّذِى هُوَ جُندٌ لَّكُمْ يَنصُرُكُم مِّن دُونِ ٱلرَّحْمَٰنِ ۚ إِنِ
ٱلْكَٰفِرُونَ إِلَّا فِى غُرُورٍ ۝ أَمَّنْ هَٰذَا ٱلَّذِى يَرْزُقُكُمْ إِنْ أَمْسَكَ
رِزْقَهُۥ ۚ بَل لَّجُّوا۟ فِى عُتُوٍّ وَنُفُورٍ ﴿٢١﴾-﴿٢٠﴾

20-21. Is this your [pathetic] army who will aid you against the Lord of Mercy, Indeed, the disbelievers are only [lost] in delusion! Who can provide for you if He withholds His provision? Yet they persist in their arrogance and aversion [to the truth].

The tone of verses 20 and 21 signals a departure from the topic of reflection and contemplation to instead deliver a shattering message which deconstructs the false beliefs and mentality of the idolaters of Makkah. The two verses challenge the prevailing belief at the time that idols such as Lāt, ʿUzza, Manāt could protect them against punishment and grant blessings and prosperity.

The two verses can be looked as a pair, each delivering a blow from different perspectives. Verse 20 deals with the idea of protection whereas verse 21 dismantles the notion that their idols could bestow blessings.

20: **Is this your [pathetic] army who will aid you against the Lord of Mercy? Indeed, the disbelievers are simply [lost] in delusion!**

21: **Who can provide for you if He withholds His provision? Yet they persist in their arrogance and aversion [to the truth].**

Verse 20 begins: **Is this your [pathetic] army who will aid you against the Lord of Mercy?** This is a rhetorical question intended to undermine the claim of the idolaters,[116] as if to say: you don't really think that these idols propped up around the Kaʿbah can help if the Almighty wanted to harm you?[117]

Other scholars such as Imām al-Rāzī interpreted **army** as a reference to the idolaters, as they perceived themselves as a force to be reckoned with due to their noble lineages, wealth, and military power.[118]

In any case, these verses may be subtly linked to verses 16 and 17 to provide a fuller sense of divine punishment, as in those earlier verses, Allāh threatened to destroy the idolaters by either causing the earth to swallow them up or by sending down a hail of stones.[119] It may have occurred in the minds of those people that, in such a scenario, they could call upon their idols to intervene and rescue them. However, here verse 20 clearly undermines that idea. It would have sent a clear message which they would have found difficult to deny as they already believed that the God who created the world was the Supreme Being and all the idols were beneath Him.

116 *Al-Taḥrīr wa Al-Tanwīr* 67:20, Ibn ʿĀshūr.

117 *Jāmiʿ al-Bayān fī Ta'wīl al-Qur'ān* 67:20, Imām al-Ṭabarī.

118 *Al-Tafsīr al-Kabīr* 67:21, al-Rāzī.

119 Verse 16 "Do you feel secure that the One Who is in heaven will not cause the earth to swallow you…" Verse 17 "Or do you feel secure that the One Who is in heaven will not unleash upon you a storm of stones…"

Moreover, the wording of the verse has been crafted such that it makes the meaning extremely overpowering and compelling.

1. Firstly, there is a sense of sarcasm created by the use of the word *man,* translated here as 'who'. It creates a dismissive tone as if to say: 'Does anybody even know *who* this army is?'

2. The verse transitions from 3rd person to the 2nd person, as in the previous verse, Allāh was speaking about the idolaters, whereas now He speaks directly to them: **Is this <u>your</u> [pathetic] army**. This adds an element of intensity, making the admonishment even more effective.[120]

3. Lastly, when speaking about the need to protect themselves against God, the name *al-Raḥmān* (The Lord of Mercy) was used. At this, one might wonder: why was the name *al-Raḥmān* chosen when speaking about punishment? The idea here is that it is solely down to the mercy of God that people are not suffering and experiencing chaos. It is His mercy that is holding back the punishment. Thus, all it would take for people to start suffering was for *al-Raḥmān* to withdraw the mercy He was showing them.

120 *Naẓm al-Durar* 67:21, al-Biqāʿī.

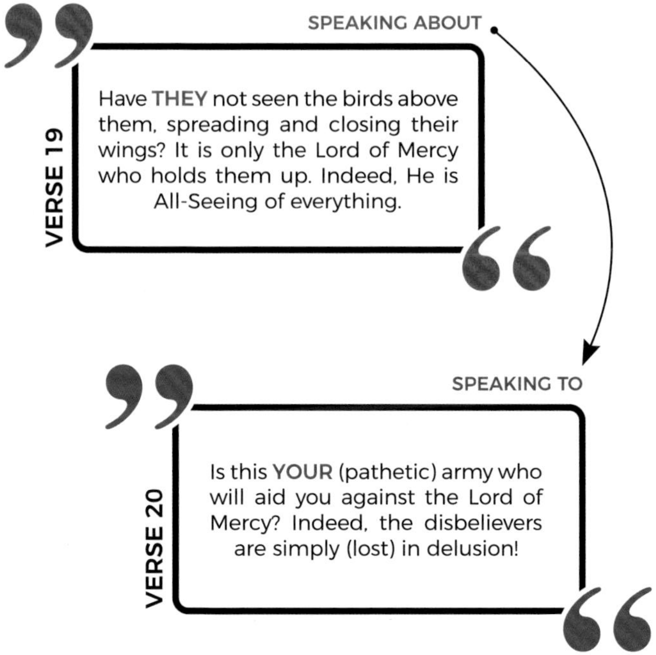

SPEAKING ABOUT
VERSE 19
Have THEY not seen the birds above them, spreading and closing their wings? It is only the Lord of Mercy who holds them up. Indeed, He is All-Seeing of everything.
SPEAKING TO
VERSE 20
Is this YOUR (pathetic) army who will aid you against the Lord of Mercy? Indeed, the disbelievers are simply (lost) in delusion!

Verse 20 concludes: **Indeed, the disbelievers are only [lost] in delusion!** This highlights the absurdity of their belief that the idols could protect them from harm.

The word translated as 'deluded' is *ghurūr*, which is being used to describe the reliance the idolaters placed in their gods to grant them protection and blessings. However, the meaning is expanded to include the broader category of **the disbelievers**, for the belief that entities beneath God have an inherent power to protect or grant blessings is in pure delusion.[121] This idea is further magnified through the use of the word *fī* ('in'), which literally means they are 'inside' delusion as if to say: they are drowning in delusion.

121 *Al-Taḥrīr wa Al-Tanwīr* 67:21, Ibn 'Āshūr.

Reflection

One of the end-goals of Iblīs (Satan) is to make people live in a state of delusion whereby their moral compass becomes so corrupt they consider good as evil and evil as good. This is a form of compounded ignorance and presents a catastrophic danger to the person as Iblīs has tricked them so cunningly that they will not even consider correcting themselves. What form of punishment could be worse than this?

The next verse (21) then undermines the idea that their idols could grant them blessings and prosperity by saying: **Who can provide for you if He withholds His provision? Yet they persist in their arrogance and aversion [to the truth].**

From His infinite wisdom, Allāh never said: "I am the only One providing for you." Instead, He chose to say: **Who can provide for you if He withholds His provision?** Not only does this establish the fact the He is the source of all goodness, wealth, and resource, but it also undermines the idea that there could possibly be another source elsewhere and that His ability to enrich someone is contingent upon another being or deity. Such a strong message is echoed elsewhere in the Qur'ān as well:

Ask [them, O Prophet], "Who provides for you from the heavens and the earth?" Say, "Allāh! Now, certainly one of our two groups is [rightly] guided; the other is clearly astray." [122]

The words: **if He withholds His provision**, educate the reader not to view wealth and resources (*rizq*) as the belonging of people, countries, or even the planet. This is because all wealth and provision are entirely His, whether He sends it down from the sky or places it in the ground. People should see themselves as merely caretakers of this wealth, entrusted with it. Who then will provide for mankind

122 Qur'ān 34:24.

should God withdraw water, or withhold air from them, or indeed any of the elements that are essential for life? If the Almighty commands the heaven to halt rainfall, plants will no longer grow on the earth, and numerous blights may destroy the cultivated lands. Then, human beings will no longer be provided with their daily sustenance.

Sayyid Quṭb brilliantly summarised the meaning of *rizq* when he said:

> Included under this are all the meanings that readily spring to mind when the term is used, and which man tends to treat as of his own making, such as work, invention, and production. All these are closely linked to primary causes on the one hand and are dependent on what God grants to individuals and communities on the other. Every breath a worker draws and every movement he experiences is part of God's provisions. Is He not the One who originated him, gave him all his abilities and powers, created for him the breath he draws in and the substance that is consumed by his body enabling movement? Every mental endeavour man makes is part of God's provision. Is He not the Creator who gave man the ability to think and invent? Besides, what can anyone produce unless he uses a substance initially made by God, and utilizes natural and human factors provided by Him?[123]

Likewise, if the spiritual provisions and Divine Revelation were to be withheld, no one would be able to guide humanity. These are evident truths that people should reflect on, but some are blinded by their ignorance and continue to persist in insolence, refusing to acknowledge the truth. Thus, the blessed verse closes by saying: **Yet they persist in their arrogance and aversion [to the truth]**.

123 *In the Shade of the Qur'ān* by Sayyid Quṭb.

The core meaning of the phrase *lajjū fī ʿutuw* is to persist and to be stubborn, but in this context, Ibn ʿĀshūr explains it as referring to stubbornness in argumentation and being extreme in rejecting anything that goes against their desires.[124] There are some people with whom you cannot have a civilised discussion about religion. They raise their voices, become very emotional, and often resort to mockery. No amount of rational talk or good manners seems to make them understand. This is how they persist in their path of darkness and refuse to listen. For such people, it is no longer about the truth but rather a matter of pride; to change now would mean to lose face and damage their image. This is the type of mentality that the verse alludes to.

Reflection

A constant theme in the Qur'ān is that Allāh the Almighty is the provider of all sustenance and that nothing in this world could add or diminish what He has decreed to reach us. People are thus enjoined to recognize that nothing truly belongs to them and to spend in charity from what God has provided them. It also reinforces the concept of *tawakkul* (trust and reliance) in Allāh and teaches us not to be excessively worried about seeking out our *rizq* (wealth and provision), for it has already been predetermined and measured out by the Almighty.

أَفَمَن يَمْشِي مُكِبًّا عَلَىٰ وَجْهِهِۦٓ أَهْدَىٰٓ أَمَّن يَمْشِي
سَوِيًّا عَلَىٰ صِرَٰطٍ مُّسْتَقِيمٍ ٢٢

22. Now, who is better guided: the one who crawls facedown or the one who walks upright on the Straight Path?

124 *Al-Taḥrīr wa Al-Tanwīr* 67:21, Ibn ʿĀshūr.

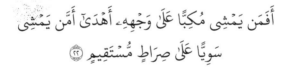

The mentality of the disbelievers has been made clear in the previous verses. They **persist in arrogance and aversion [to the truth]** (verse 21), and they **are truly deluded** (verse 20). *Sūrah al-Mulk* now projects that mentality in the form of an image for all to see. Moreover, it compares it with a starkly contrasting image of a believer.

This is framed within another rhetorical question: **Now, who is [rightly] guided?** Though the answer to the question is clear, the description of each type of person makes something else become abundantly clear: the huge difference between walking the path of guidance vis-à-vis the path of misguidance.

As for the disbeliever, he **crawls facedown** (*yamshī mukibban ʿalā wajh*) when walking his chosen path. As for the believer, he **walks upright on the Straight Path.**

The phrase *yamshī mukibban ʿalā wajh,* translated as **crawls facedown**, can be understood as referring to a person who is walking along a very uneven path where the ground is so unstable and rough that it causes the person to trip and fall facedown repeatedly.[125] To visualise this, think of a time where you tried walking along a stream, balancing on the slippery pebbles. It was likely impossible to walk upright or move about without tripping.

Other Qur'ānic commentators have said that this phrase depicts an image of the blind trying to walk and find their way without any guide—at some point they are bound to trip up.[126] In any case, the imagery vividly illustrates the disbelievers' state of spiritual ruin. It is so poor that the person lives without direction, constantly falling into problems. Whichever way they turn in search of happiness and contentment, they stumble and find themselves at a loss. They may get back up, eager to find happiness in another endeavour, only to fall there too. This pattern

125 *Al-Tafsīr al-Kabīr* 67:22, al-Rāzī.
126 *Al-Jāmiʿ li-Aḥkām al-Qur'ān* 67:22, by al-Qurṭubī.

of life thus develops into a continuous loop, a cycle of unhappiness. The opposite is true for a believer; with every step they take to learn and practice the teachings of Islam they feel more and more content, they gain more meaning in life and ultimately become stronger.

Contrasting this image with that of a believer, the verse says he **walks upright on the Straight Path**—a path that is smooth and stable to walk on. The adjective **Straight** is translated as *mustaqīm*, which means elevated without any turns or crookedness, thereby allowing the person to stand upright without fear of falling or tripping.[127] In this phrase: **walks upright on the Straight Path**, both the person and the path they traverse are described as being upright (*sawiyy*) and straight (*mustaqīm*), respectively. The implication is that the **Straight Path** of Islam is easy to traverse, elevates the one traversing it, and causes a transformation in their character, thus making them **upright** (*sawiyy*). Their journey is, therefore, one of progress and advancement. On the other hand, the disbeliever's path is crooked and bent, so even when plenty of effort is made to walk it, they may not be any closer to their goal than had they remained idle.

Another more literal view has been put forward by the Successor Qatādah (d. 118H) and others. According to this view, the meaning relates to the Afterlife and explains a form of punishment that will be meted out to the disbelievers.[128] These scholars say that the disbeliever will be gathered on the Day of Judgement with his face forced to the ground. A Prophetic narration is cited to support this view where the Prophet ﷺ was asked, 'How will the disbeliever be made to walk on their face?' The Prophet ﷺ responded, 'The One who made them walk on their feet in this world is capable of making them walk on their faces in the Afterlife.'[129]

---

127 *Al-Kashshāf* 67:22, al-Zamakhsharī.
128 *Jāmiʿ al-Bayān fī Taʾwīl al-Qurʾān* 67:22, Imām al-Ṭabarī.
129 Ibid.

Word Bank
Section Three Verses 13–22

VERSE 15

ذَلُولًا

Dhalūl

The word dhalūl is normally used to describe an animal that has been tamed. Its core-meaning (dhull) revolves around the idea of subjugation and being humbled. In verse 15 it is used to describe the earth's nature as one by which people can use it to serve their own interests despite it being greater in size and tougher than them

VERSE 21

لَّجُّوا۟ فِى عُتُوٍّ

Lajjū fī ʿutuw

The phrase lajjū fī ʿutuw means to persist and to be stubborn. In the context of verse 21 Ibn ʿĀshūr explains it as referring to stubbornness in argumentation and being extreme in rejecting anything that goes against their desires.

VERSE 22

يَمْشِى مُكِبًّا عَلَىٰ وَجْهِهِۦ

Yamshī mukibban ʿalā wajh

The phrase yamshī mukibban ʿalā wajh, translated as crawls facedown, can be understood as referring to a person who's walking along a very uneven path where the ground is so unstable and rough that it causes the person to trip and fall facedown repeatedly.

الملك

Section Four

Verses 23–24

Life is short & time is running out

Section Four [Verses 23-24]

Life is Short & Time is Running Out

The message in section 3 revolved around giving warnings to the stubborn and spiritually blind. This section underscores that message by alerting them to the fleeting nature of this life to create a sense of urgency to heed those warnings. This is how section 3 graciously transitions into section 4.

The shortness of this section, being only two verses long, reflects its message: Life is short and time is running out.

In these two verses—23 and 24—the entire life cycle of a human being on this earth is summarised. Youthfulness is quickly overtaken by old age, and the faculties of sight, hearing, and intellect, which we rely on to enjoy life, quickly diminish and undergo a reversal back to childhood. This should then create a sense of urgency within the reader to change and improve themselves in order to prepare for their inevitable meeting with Allāh.

Section Four Verses 23–24
Life is short & time is running out

23. Say, [O Prophet,] "He is the One Who brought you into being and gave you hearing, sight, and intellect. [Yet] you hardly give any thanks."	قُلْ هُوَ الَّذِىٓ أَنشَأَكُمْ وَجَعَلَ لَكُمُ السَّمْعَ وَالْأَبْصَارَ وَالْأَفْـِٔدَةَ ۖ قَلِيلًا مَّا تَشْكُرُونَ ﴿٢٣﴾
24. [Also] say, "He is the One Who has dispersed you [all] over the earth, and to Him you will [all] be gathered."	قُلْ هُوَ ٱلَّذِى ذَرَأَكُمْ فِى ٱلْأَرْضِ وَإِلَيْهِ تُحْشَرُونَ ﴿٢٤﴾

قُلْ هُوَ الَّذِىٓ أَنشَأَكُمْ وَجَعَلَ لَكُمُ السَّمْعَ وَالْأَبْصَارَ
وَالْأَفْـِٔدَةَ ۖ قَلِيلًا مَّا تَشْكُرُونَ ﴿٢٣﴾

23. Say, [O Prophet,] "He is the One Who brought you into being and gave you hearing, sight, and intellect. [Yet] you hardly give any thanks."

The basic meaning of this verse is that Allāh alone deserves your ultimate thanks and worship, and that no other entity or person in your life should be loved and feared as much as the Almighty. The way in which this message is communicated makes it all the more compelling. The Prophet ﷺ is told to declare that Allāh is the only One who has bestowed four blessings upon humanity, namely:

1. Brought us into being.
2. Gave us the faculty of hearing.
3. Blessed us with sight.
4. Gifted us intellect.

This should create an extra sense of importance within the heart of the listener, for the Prophet of God ﷺ only speaks the truth and conveys spiritual knowledge that contains no doubt. All four relate to blessings that we carry within us, as opposed to the blessings around us, such as the beauty of a flawless starlit sky or an easily traversable earth, both of which have already been mentioned earlier in *Sūrah al-Mulk*.[130]

The order of the blessings also contains wisdom. By first stating that Allāh was the One who brought **you into being,** it suggests that of the four, the gift of life is the greatest. As for the other three, it is as if to say that Allāh went further to complete that favour of life by gifting the human being with faculties by which they can experience and enjoy it. The ability to hear, see, and understand allows life to become meaningful and purposeful. Moreover, they enable the person to discover the Signs of Allāh and follow the Straight Path.[131] Thus, the wisdom in positioning this verse after a series of verses in which warnings and serious counsel were given becomes clear. Verse 19 told the critic to look at the flight of birds and see the Signs of God. Verses 16, 17, and 18 told them to recall the devastating divine punishment that came to perished nations, something the Quraysh of Makkah would have heard about. Finally, verses 20 and 21 furnished rational proofs to show the fallacy of idol worship. Therefore, all three faculties listed here in verse 23—hearing, sight, and intellect—are neatly synced with the verses that precede it.

130 Qur'ān 67:3-5.

131 *Rūḥ al-Maʿānī fī Tafsīr al-Qur'ān al-ʿAẓīm wa'l-Sabʿ al-Mathānī* 67:23, by al-Ālūsī.

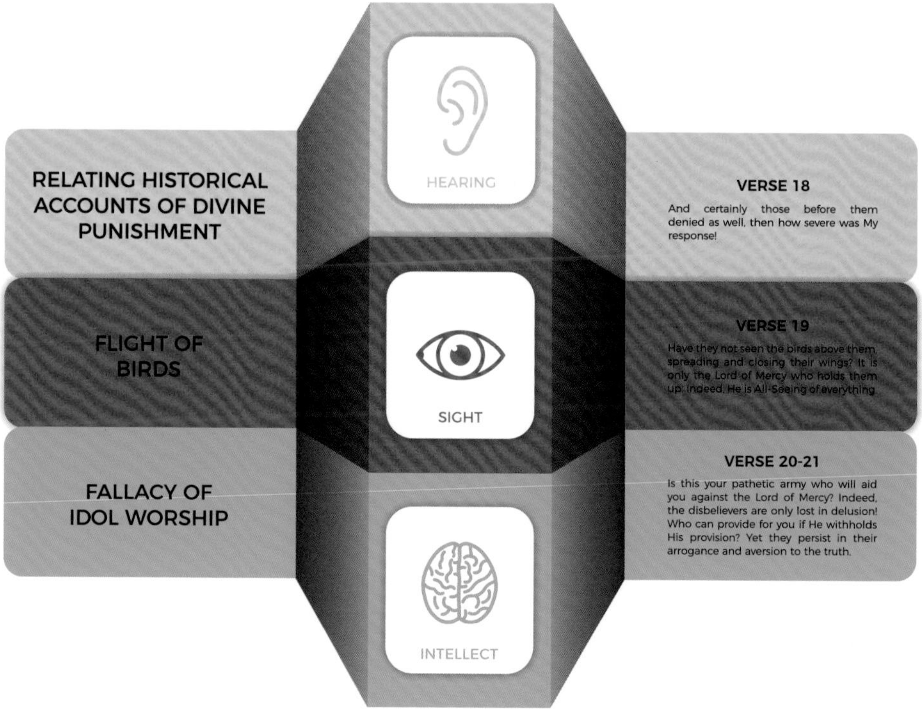

Figure 10: The 3 human faculties listed in verse 23 & their connection with previous verses

As for the compelling aspect, these four blessings are undeniably and exclusively from God and not the idols. The Quraysh, though bent on disbelieving in Muḥammad ﷺ, would have had no choice but to recognise this fact, as part of their theology, was the belief in Allāh as the sole creator.[132]

132 *Al-Jāmiʿ li-Aḥkām al-Qurʾān* 67:23, by al-Qurṭubī.

When contrasting this verse with the previous verses, we notice two points of distinction. Firstly, Allāh is no longer talking to the disbelievers directly, but through the blessed lips of His Messenger using the instruction *qul,* 'say' i.e. say on My behalf. This creates a sense of variety in speech which serves to heighten the interest of the reader. Secondly, the threatening tone and message of warning have been replaced with a softer call to reflect over the blessings of God and arrive at the station of faith. Lastly, the instruction to the Prophet ﷺ to speak (*qul*) elevates his position and rank as he is being given an opportunity to speak alongside God.

The verse ends almost abruptly: **[Yet] you hardly give any thanks.** This is as if to say that despite such love and generosity, people still do not thank God as much as they ought to—a claim that could easily be made against many of us. In fact, some scholars explain that *qalīlan mā tashkurūn* is a figure of speech (*kināyah*) to mean: they give absolutely no thanks!

The conclusive remark, when understood in the context of the Quraysh refusing to worship God alone, illustrates a powerful lesson often repeated in the Qur'ān. The idea of worshiping God (*ʿibādah*) and being grateful to Him (*shukr*) are frequently used interchangeably. The reason for this is to show that the correct manner in which to show gratitude to God is to devote yourself in worship to Him alone without partners. Conversely, people can never consider themselves as true worshippers of God if they constantly fail to appreciate His blessings and are ungrateful towards Him. Compare this now with the kind of gratitude that the Prophet ﷺ would show to Allāh. Whilst prostrating facedown on the ground, he would utter, "I have prostrated my face to the One who created it, fashioned it, and endowed it with the ability to hear and see."

Reflection

One of the most amazing praises given to Prophet Noah in the Qur'ān is when Allāh declares: *He was indeed a grateful servant.*[133] The reason I find this fascinating is because Noah struggled in his mission to help people find God for almost a thousand years. When a person exerts great effort for a cause and sees little results, they often lose hope and blame God for a lack of support. Now imagine the case if the mission was undertaken because of God's direct instruction. Noah struggled for 950 years with only 80-odd people following him, and yet he remained committed to God, always thanking him for His favours. May Allāh make us from the few who truly thank Him.

قُلْ هُوَ ٱلَّذِى ذَرَأَكُمْ فِى ٱلْأَرْضِ وَإِلَيْهِ تُحْشَرُونَ ﴿٢٤﴾

24. [Also] say, "He is the One Who has dispersed you [all] over the earth, and to Him you will [all] be gathered."

This verse can be interpreted to mean that Allāh is the One who allowed you to flourish in great numbers on the earth[134]; which was already explained as having been made smooth and vast for humanity.[135] It can also mean that Allāh has distributed human beings throughout the various regions of the planet and, despite their different languages, colours, shapes, appearances, and forms, Allāh will surely gather them all together on a single plane on the Day of Judgement for a reckoning.[136] The extra pronoun 'He' (*huwa*) creates a double emphasis on Allāh being the sole reason why human beings flourish on the earth with such diversity. Again, as if to echo the point made in the previous verse, it stresses the lack of appreciation people have for the role God plays in their lives.

---

133 Qur'ān 17:3.

134 *Rūḥ al-Maʿānī fī Tafsīr al-Qur'ān al-ʿAẓīm wa'l-Sabʿ al-Mathānī* 67:24, by al-Ālūsī.

135 Qur'ān 67:15.

136 *Tafsīr al-Qur'ān al-ʿAẓīm* 67:24, Ibn Kathīr.

The word **dispersed** translates the Arabic word *dhara'a,* which originally means to become old or refers to hair turning grey.[137] The meaning would thus be that Allāh is the One who causes people to live to see old age and experience its weaknesses and frailty. This would contrast with the previous verse (23), which says **He is the One Who brought you into being** (*ansha'a*), as the word *ansha'a* means to nurture something to grow and rise. The two verses therefore complete the picture of care that Allāh shows to humanity. The format of the verse is also identical: "Say He is the One who", thereby inviting the reader to compare and contrast the two verses.

The word *dhara'a* can also mean to sow into the earth.[138] The meaning would then refer to the final resting place of people being inside the earth, buried in the soil like a seed. However, death is not the end. As the last part of the verse states, **and to Him you will [all] be gathered**. People will arise back up out of the earth for a reckoning.

Verses 23 and 24 summarise the entire life cycle of a human being on this earth, and the brevity with which the verses do this reflects the shortness of this worldly life. In the blink of an eye, youthfulness is overtaken by old age, and the faculties of sight, hearing, and intellect, which we rely on to enjoy life (as mentioned in verse 23), begin to deteriorate. This realisation creates a sense of urgency within the reader to change and improve themselves in preparation for their unavoidable meeting with Allāh.

137 *Mufradāt Alfāẓ al-Qur'ān,* entry ذرأ, al-Rāghib al-Aṣfahānī.
138 *Al-Muʿjam al-Ishtiqāqī,* entry ذرأ, Muḥammad Ḥasan Jabal.

الملك

Section Five

Verses 25–27

Those who reject the Afterlife

Section Five [Verses 25-27]

Those who reject the Afterlife

Instead of heeding the warnings laid out in section 3 and recognising that the time for change was running out (section 4), many of the idolaters of Makkah refused to listen to the Prophet ﷺ. This is why section 5 speaks about the final destiny of those who reject belief in the Afterlife. From this perspective, section 5 is a mirror image of section 2, which also dealt with the reality of the Afterlife. It can also be seen as a completion of section 2, as section 5 depicts the reaction and even the facial expressions of those who rejected the Afterlife on the Day of Judgement when Hell is brought before their very eyes. *Then when they see the torment drawing near, the faces of the disbelievers will become distressed, and it will be said [to them], "This is what you claimed would never come."* (Verse 27.)

Section Five Verses 25–27
Those who reject the Afterlife

25. [Still] they ask [the believers], "When will this threat come to pass, if what you say is really true?"	وَيَقُولُونَ مَتَىٰ هَـٰذَا ٱلْوَعْدُ إِن كُنتُمْ صَـٰدِقِينَ ﴿٢٥﴾
26. Say, [O Prophet,] "God alone has knowledge of this, and I am only sent with a clear warning."	قُلْ إِنَّمَا ٱلْعِلْمُ عِندَ ٱللَّهِ وَإِنَّمَآ أَنَا نَذِيرٌ مُّبِينٌ ﴿٢٦﴾
27. Then when they see the torment drawing near, the faces of the disbelievers will become distressed, and it will be said [to them], "This is what you claimed would never come."	فَلَمَّا رَأَوْهُ زُلْفَةً سِيٓـَٔتْ وُجُوهُ ٱلَّذِينَ كَفَرُوا۟ وَقِيلَ هَـٰذَا ٱلَّذِى كُنتُم بِهِۦ تَدَّعُونَ ﴿٢٧﴾

وَيَقُولُونَ مَتَىٰ هَٰذَا ٱلْوَعْدُ إِن كُنتُمْ صَٰدِقِينَ
قُلْ إِنَّمَا ٱلْعِلْمُ عِندَ ٱللَّهِ وَإِنَّمَآ أَنَا۠ نَذِيرٌ مُّبِينٌ ﴿٢٥-٢٦﴾

25-26. [Still] they ask [the believers], "When will this threat come to pass, if what you say is really true?" Say, [O Prophet,] "God alone has knowledge of this, and I am only sent with a clear warning."

The Prophet ﷺ and his Companions were consistent in their message, repeatedly reminding the people about the coming of the Day of Judgement. They were not too shy or afraid to give genuine counsel to their communities and relate the warnings of the Qur'ān about the Afterlife. We know this to be the case because of instances like verse 25 which highlight the response the Muslims would receive when they would try to share such warnings: **"When will this threat come to pass, if what you say is really true?"**

Even in their persistent denial of the resurrection, they still constantly asked about its timing. However, this was not a sincere question. The critics of the Prophet ﷺ were not at all truly curious about when the final hour would come to pass, but instead, they mocked him and showed their disdain for the whole idea of human resurrection. It could also be seen as their way of daring the Prophet ﷺ as if to say 'let's see it then, bring it!'[139] This can be gleaned from the subtle indications of the Arabic wording of the verse.

Firstly, the word *yaqūlūna* (**they ask**) appears in the present tense, which carries a sense of repetition,[140] as if to say that they would repeatedly use this question to bat away the warnings about the Afterlife. As a secondary point, this also highlights the frequency in which the Muslims would go

139 *Al-Muḥarrar al-Wajīz* 67:25, Ibn ʿAṭiyyah.
140 *Al-Taḥrīr wa Al-Tanwīr* 67:25, Ibn ʿĀshūr.

out of their way to remind them about the Afterlife— something rarely seen in modern times.

Secondly, their saying **if what you say is really true?** is meant to cast doubt on the integrity of the Muslims. The implication being: you people cannot be trusted in any case, so how then can we take your word about such a great piece of news or promise from God?

Thirdly, the very nature of the question shows they were not interested in finding out whether or not resurrection and the Afterlife was a reality, for how would being told the exact timing of the final hour prove whether or not it was going to happen? It would be the equivalent of refusing to accept a pandemic will reach you unless the experts could tell you the exact time it would arrive.

In any case, a response is given in the next verse: **Say, [O Prophet,] "God alone has knowledge of this, and I am only sent with a clear warning."** The Prophet ﷺ is told to respond to this question and say that despite being a Prophet of God, even he does not know when the final hour will arrive. In fact, it is not even part of his role to know this for he is told to say: **I am only sent with a clear warning**, meaning he is only a warner meant to deliver this warning and open the eyes of humanity to the truth.[141]

The style of the answer employs a rhetorical tool known as the 'riddle in response',[142] as the answer does not address the question with an expected response, but rather something else which would come as a surprise to the questioner. They asked *when* the final hour will occur, and in response, they are told that God knows and the Prophet ﷺ is simply a warner. This response contains wisdom. A straight answer would have validated the question as if it were a reasonable one, when it is clear that

141 *Tafsīr al-Qur'ān al-ʿAẓīm* 67:26, Ibn Kathīr.
142 It is known as *uslūb al-ḥakīm* in Arabic rhetoric.

any form of validation was undeserved due to the insincerity with which it was asked. Effectively, Allāh is saying: it is not the *when* that should be your concern, as this is an undeniable fact, rather your concern should be what you are doing to prepare for that monumental day.

Elsewhere, the Qur'ān responds to the same question with a similarly wise answer. It is asked: *When will this threat come to pass, if what you say is true?* To which the Qur'ān responds: *Say O Prophet "A Day has [already] been appointed for you, which you can neither delay nor advance by a [single] moment".*[143] In both of these responses, the Prophet ﷺ is being taught not to dignify the foolish with straight answers, and not to allow them to side-track him from his mission. This then becomes a lesson for all Muslims on how to tackle awkward questions posed by critics and those with ulterior motives.

فَلَمَّا رَأَوْهُ زُلْفَةً سِيٓـَٔتْ وُجُوهُ ٱلَّذِينَ كَفَرُوا۟ وَقِيلَ
هَـٰذَا ٱلَّذِى كُنتُم بِهِۦ تَدَّعُونَ ﴿٢٧﴾

27. Then when they see the torment drawing near, the faces of the disbelievers will become distressed, and it will be said [to them], "This is what you claimed would never come."

The *Sūrah* now presents an image depicting the threat mentioned in verse 26 to conclude the response to their sinister question in verse 25: *"When will this threat come to pass, if what you say is really true?"*

The verse seamlessly transports the critics into the future to see the *threat* which they doubt unfold before their very eyes: **Then when they see the torment drawing near, the faces of the disbelievers will become distressed.**

143 Qur'ān 34:30.

The Qur'ān often uses this method of depicting the future as if it is unfolding now in the present. The purpose, in contexts such as these, is to counter the state of doubt with an element of surprise. The critics are shown an image of the moment when they will finally realise they were wrong and have to come to terms with the consequences of having doubted such a thing. This is easy for Allāh to describe as there exists no gap in time separating the Afterlife from the present. Unlike the human being, the Final Day is present in His knowledge and is within His sight. As Allāh says elsewhere in the Qur'ān: *They truly see this [Day] as being distant, but We see it as near.*[144]

The Almighty describes the reaction on the disbelievers' faces the moment **when they see the torment drawing near.** The English translates the sentence in the future tense, whereas the Arabic (*ra'awhu*) is in fact in the past tense. This is part of the eloquence of the Qur'ān as using the past tense to speak about the future creates a sense of guarantee,[145] as if to say: **when they will see the torment** (and they most certainly will). This indicates that this future event should be viewed with as much certainty as an event that has already taken place in the past.

On that day they will be made to see the horrors of the Day of Judgement and the punishments that await them **drawing near**. The Arabic *zulfah,* translated here as 'drawing near', means to be brought so close to something that you come face-to-face with it.[146] The implication is that during this life they were heedless, negligent of the Afterlife and the warnings of punishment, but on that Day their eyes will be forced to stare at the horrors they tried their best to ignore, and their hearts will become consumed by the experience. Allāh then says: **the faces of the disbelievers will become distressed**, which brings to mind an image of faces mangled in fright and dread. The word used to describe their faces

144 Qur'an 70:6-7.
145 *Al-Taḥrīr wa Al-Tanwīr* 67:27, Ibn ʿĀshūr.
146 Ibid.

is *sī'at*, which comes from the root word *sū'*, meaning evil, disgraceful, and foul.[147] The verse explains that the faces of the disbelievers will take on such expressions due to the horror of seeing all the forms of punishment and torture that await them. In another verse of the Qur'ān, we find more detail: *And on that day some faces will be gloomy, anticipating something devastating to befall them.*[148] And in another verse: *On that Day some faces will be bright while others gloomy. To the gloomy-faced it will be said, "Did you disbelieve after having believed? So taste the punishment for your disbelief."*[149]

The verse ends by stating that such people will be interrogated[150] simultaneously by the gatekeepers of Hell[151] [152]: **and it will be said [to them], "This is what you claimed would never come"**, meaning this is what you used to arrogantly claim was a myth.[153] Another view is that **what you claimed** means: what you used to repeatedly dare the Prophet ﷺ to hasten.[154]

The phrase: **This is what you claimed would never come**, contains an added layer of emphasis created by the word order. In Arabic, the sequence of the wording would normally place the preposition and pronoun (*jār/majrūr*) at the end, whereas here the Qur'ānic verse places it earlier.

147 *Al-Muʿjam al-Ishtiqāqī al-Mu'aṣṣal* by Muḥammad Ḥasan Jabal.
148 Qur'ān 75:24-25.
149 Qur'ān 3: 106.
150 *Al-Tafsīr al-Kabīr* 67:27, al-Rāzī.
151 *Al-Taḥrīr wa Al-Tanwīr* 67:27, Ibn ʿĀshūr.
152 Another view reported by Imām al-Rāzī is that the disbelievers will say this to each other.
153 *Naẓm al-Durar* 67:27, al-Biqāʿī.
154 *Tafsīr al-Qur'ān al-ʿAẓīm* 67:27, Ibn Kathīr.

This is a rhetorical device known as *taqdīm*, and it shifts the focus of the reader to the words that are brought earlier.[155] The translation can now be modified to capture this nuance: **and it will be said [to them], "Of all things this is what you claimed would never come."**

NORMAL WORD SEQUENCE

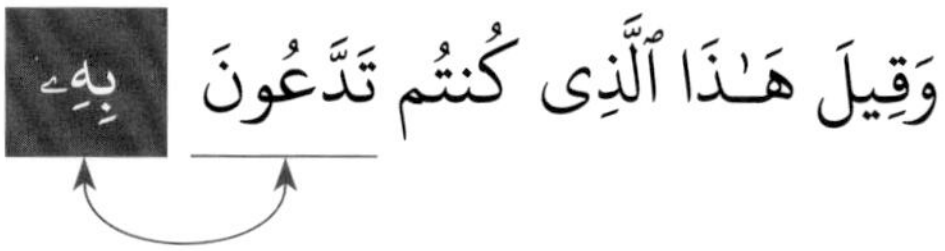

ACTUAL SEQUENCE IN THE QUR'ĀN

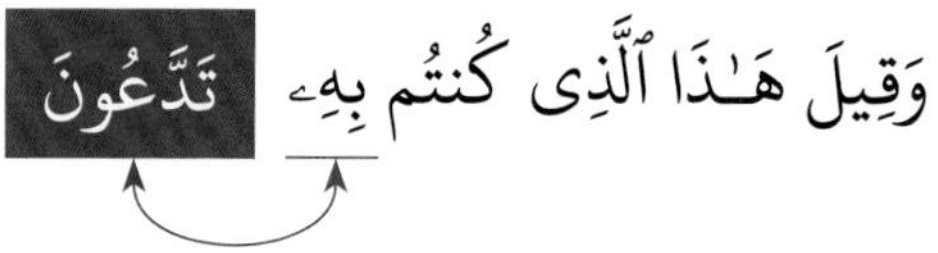

And with that, the wise response to their question is now drawn to a close. The last part of the previous verse stated that the Prophet ﷺ is **only sent with a clear warning**, and this verse aptly illustrates this warning with great clarity.

155 *Al-Taḥrīr wa Al-Tanwīr* 67:27, Ibn ʿĀshūr.

Word Bank

Section Five Verses 25–27

زُلْفَةً

Zulfa

VERSE 27

The word zulfa, translated as 'drawing near', means to be brought so close to something you come face-to-face with it.

سِيٓـَٔتْ وُجُوهُ

Sī'at wujūh

VERSE 27

The phrase sī'at wujūh means 'distressed face', where the word sī'at comes from the root word sū', meaning evil, disgraceful and foul. This is a reference to how the faces of the disbelievers will appear on the Day of Judgement due to the horror of seeing the forms of punishment and torture that await them.

الملك

Section Six

Verses 28–30

People are weak

Section Six [Verses 28-30]
People are weak

In this final section, Allāh's power is contrasted with human weakness, creating a climactic ending to the *Sūrah*, which pairs beautifully with the beginning of the *Sūrah*. At the end of the first verse, we are told that Allāh 'is Most Capable of everything', and in the last verse, it shows that if He wished He could cut the supply of fresh water to the planet, leaving people in desperation and helplessness. The underlying message is then to appreciate the greatness of Allāh by reflecting on humanity's weaknesses and our total dependency on the Almighty.

Section Six Verses 28–30
People are weak

28. Say, [O Prophet,] "Just think- regardless of whether God destroys me and my followers or has mercy on us- who will protect the disbelievers from an agonizing torment?"	قُلْ أَرَءَيْتُمْ إِنْ أَهْلَكَنِيَ ٱللَّهُ وَمَن مَّعِيَ أَوْ رَحِمَنَا فَمَن يُجِيرُ ٱلْكَـٰفِرِينَ مِنْ عَذَابٍ أَلِيمٍ ﴿٢٨﴾
29. Say, [O Prophet,] "He is the Lord of Mercy—we believe in Him, and in Him [alone] we trust. You will soon come to know who is clearly astray."	قُلْ هُوَ ٱلرَّحْمَـٰنُ ءَامَنَّا بِهِۦ وَعَلَيْهِ تَوَكَّلْنَا ۖ فَسَتَعْلَمُونَ مَنْ هُوَ فِى ضَلَـٰلٍ مُّبِينٍ ﴿٢٩﴾
30. Say, [O Prophet,] "If all your water were to disappear into the earth who could give you flowing water in its place?"	قُلْ أَرَءَيْتُمْ إِنْ أَصْبَحَ مَآؤُكُمْ غَوْرًا فَمَن يَأْتِيكُم بِمَآءٍ مَّعِينٍ ﴿٣٠﴾

قُلۡ أَرَءَيۡتُمۡ إِنۡ أَهۡلَكَنِيَ ٱللَّهُ وَمَن مَّعِيَ أَوۡ رَحِمَنَا فَمَن يُجِيرُ
ٱلۡكَٰفِرِينَ مِنۡ عَذَابٍ أَلِيمٖ ۝٢٨

28. Say, [O Prophet,] "Just think- regardless of whether God destroys me and my followers or has mercy on us- who will protect the disbelievers from an agonizing torment?"

After a graphic description of the punishment in the Afterlife, *Sūrah al-Mulk* shifts the focus back to the life of this world, issuing three further instructions to the Prophet ﷺ to challenge his critics.

The first threat is delivered through a rhetorical question carrying a sense of contempt:[156] **Say, [O Prophet,] "Just think- regardless of whether God destroys me and my followers or has mercy on us- who will protect the disbelievers from an agonizing torment?"** The basis for this was the repulsive behaviour that the idolaters of Makkah showed the Prophet ﷺ. They saw him as a form of bad luck, an irritation, and would sometimes publicly wish death upon the Prophet ﷺ along with all his followers,[157] hoping that they would simply leave them alone. Some of them even plotted to assassinate the Prophet ﷺ and attempted it on more than one occasion. In another verse Allāh informs us: *Or do they say, "[He is] a poet, for whom we [eagerly] await an ill-fate!"?*[158]

With this context in mind, the verse is making a point that even if their wishes were to come true, and they managed to silence him, it would not at all affect the outcome of their fate with God. This is because people are taken to account based on their faith and lifestyle; the presence or absence of other people in their life, even a prophet of God, will not alter this reality. This implies that the problem in this situation lies not with

156 *Al-Taḥrīr wa Al-Tanwīr* 67:28, Ibn ʿĀshūr.
157 *Irshād al-ʿAql al-Salīm* 67:28, Abū al-Saʿūd.
158 Qur'ān 52:30.

the Prophet ﷺ but rather with his critics, such that even if the Prophet ﷺ was taken out of the picture, it would not change the fact that they would have to answer to Allāh for their crimes. A similar point is echoed elsewhere in the Qur'ān where Allāh says *Even if We take you away [from this world], We will surely inflict punishment upon them.*[159]

There is a sense of familiarity between this verse and the previous ones in which we observe the idolaters daring the Prophet ﷺ to hasten the punishment just to see if it was really true. In both cases, the disbelievers are being hasty, either about the Day of Judgement (verse 25) or about wanting the Prophet ﷺ to die so they could live in peace (verse 28), and in both cases, the response is: Your hastiness will not benefit you nor help you in any way. If the punishment were brought forward sooner, you would suffer a horrible fate, and if the Prophet ﷺ were to pass away early, your path to salvation would be cut off, whereas the rewards that await him will be brought forward, much to his delight. Such intra-*Sūrah* connections further highlight the divine arrangement of the Qur'ān.

Point of benefit

The Tunisian scholar Ibn 'Āshūr points out the contrast between destruction (*ihlāk)* and mercy (*raḥmah*) as stated in the verse: **regardless of whether God destroys** (*ihlāk)* **me and my followers or has mercy** (*raḥmah*) **on us.** This alludes to the fact that when Allāh grants someone a long life, it is considered an act of mercy and a divine blessing. Although the verse speaks about the hypothetical scenario in which the Prophet ﷺ either dies or is kept alive, we find that the word mercy (*raḥmah*) is used instead of 'kept alive', thus signalling this idea of a long life being an expression of God's mercy and favour due to the opportunities it provides one to engage in more good deeds.[160]

159 Qur'ān 43:41.
160 *Al-Taḥrīr wa Al-Tanwīr* 67:28, Ibn 'Āshūr.

LIFE MERCY DEATH PUNISHMENT

قُلْ أَرَءَيْتُمْ إِنْ أَهْلَكَنِيَ ٱللَّهُ وَمَن مَّعِيَ أَوْ رَحِمَنَا

Regardless of whether Allah
destroys me and my followers
or lets us live has mercy on us

Reflection

The Prophet ﷺ was the nicest, kindest person in the world and yet there were people who despised him and wished death upon him. This teaches us that some people's hatred is irrational and in no way a reflection of a shortcoming within you. Think about it. The Prophet's conduct was such that it gave people absolutely no reason to hate him but some did, and with a passion! You know why? Because his character and message was winning the hearts of the sincere, and no amount of money or torture would make his Companions leave Islam. That is why they couldn't stand him. He had something that money couldn't buy: a loving-message from the Almighty that won the hearts of people.

There is another interpretation of this verse offered by scholars such as al-Wāḥidī.[161] According to them, the statement: **regardless of whether God destroys me and my followers or has mercy on us**, is understood as referring to the fate of Believers in the Afterlife. The meaning of the next part of the verse—**who will protect the disbelievers from an agonizing torment?**— would then change to mean: if Allāh were to destroy the Believers in the Afterlife due to the mistakes they have committed,

161 *Al-Tafsīr al-Basīṭ* 67:28, al-Wāḥidī.

then what chance would the idolaters have of salvation? The implied meaning here is that even the Prophet ﷺ and his Companions felt a degree of fear and trepidation about their fate with God, despite having faith in Him. How tragic is it then that those who have strayed far away from Him don't feel any sense of worry about their fate in the Afterlife?

قُلْ هُوَ ٱلرَّحْمَـٰنُ ءَامَنَّا بِهِۦ وَعَلَيْهِ تَوَكَّلْنَا ۖ فَسَتَعْلَمُونَ
مَنْ هُوَ فِى ضَلَـٰلٍ مُّبِينٍ ﴿٢٩﴾

29. Say, [O Prophet,] "He is the Lord of Mercy—
we believe in Him, and in Him [alone] we trust.
You will soon come to know who is clearly astray."

Again, the Prophet ﷺ is told to respond to his critics who tried their best to undermine him and his followers. This time he is told to make a bold declaration: **Say, [O Prophet,] "He is the Lord of Mercy—we believe in Him, and in Him [alone] we trust. You will soon come to know who is clearly astray."**

This verse is paired with the previous one, as if to say, the reason why Allāh will not destroy me (the Prophet ﷺ) and my followers is because **we believe in Him, and in Him [alone] we trust**. As such, it can be read as a veiled threat against the disbelievers as they refused to do this, leaving themselves open to Divine punishment.[162]

The meaning of this verse ties to the previous one, which clarified that being given a long life is an expression of Allāh's mercy and that an early death for the Prophet ﷺ or him living a full life will have no bearing on the fate of his enemies. This verse builds on the idea of life being an act of mercy and explains that the reason why Allāh *would* grant someone

162 *Al-Jāmiʿ li-Aḥkām al-Qur'ān* 67:29, by al-Qurṭubī.

a long life is because of the fact that they have faith and place their trust in Him. In fact, Allāh will grant them a double portion of His mercy, one in this life and another in the Afterlife. The opposite is subtly being implied to the disbelievers[163] for their denial and rebellion deprives them of the mercy of Allāh. This will soon become clear to them, hence the verse ends: **You will soon come to know who is clearly astray.** This verse can also be understood as a form of reassurance to the believers who may have doubted themselves in this life as they faced a barrage of hate and mockery. They will also **come to know** how right they were and how wrong the others were.

The Arabic phrase **in Him [alone] we trust** contains a rhetorical feature where the word sequence is altered from the normal sequence to create a sense of exclusivity; hence the appearance of 'alone in parentheses.[164] The exclusivity created suggests that true believers ought to pin their hopes in Allāh and nothing else, unlike disbelievers who tended to place it in entities beneath God. Without this feature, the normal sequence would translate to *we trust in Him* vis-à-vis *in Him [alone] we trust*, a meaning which leaves itself open to the suggestion that they may trust in others along with Him, i.e. *we trust in Him but others too.* This belief is in stark contrast to the idolaters of Makkah who would place their hopes of happiness and prosperity in their idols, their wealth,[165] and their own abilities. Hoping in Allāh and thinking positively about Him is, therefore, a defining feature of Islamic creed. This positivity is reflected in the fact that God is referred to as **the Lord of Mercy**, where mercy expresses His love, care, and compassion towards humanity.

Interestingly, the same nuance of exclusivity does not appear when speaking about having faith in Allāh: **we believe in Him, and in Him [alone] we trust**. It is important to note that the word 'alone' does not

163 *al-Kashshāf* 67:29, al-Zamakhsharī.
164 See the explanation of verse 27 for further details.
165 *al-Kashshāf* 67:29, al-Zamakhsharī.

appear in the translation when belief is mentioned. The reason for this is that Allāh expects people to have faith in a number of things alongside Him, such as the Angels, the Afterlife, the divinely revealed scriptures, and so on. However, when it comes to trust and reliance (*tawakkul*), one should only place it in Allāh. Even when relying on people, which is permissible, one should recognise that such people are only a means through which Allāh is helping you.

Lastly, the great scholar Imām al-Saʿdī explained that having trust in Allāh is already included in the declaration: **we believe in Him**, as believing in Allāh necessarily implies believing that He alone has the power to help you.[166] The reason it was mentioned separately was to underline its importance and to raise our estimation of its value. People fail to trust in Allāh as He deserves to be trusted. The significance of trusting in God is further emphasised elsewhere in the Qur'ān, where the Almighty says: *God loves those who put their trust in Him*.[167]

Reflection

This verse instructs the Prophet ﷺ to tell the enemies of Islam that **"He is the Lord of Mercy"**. Despite them not having proper faith in God and refusing to worship Him alone, they are still told to perceive their Creator as the One who is kind, caring, and compassionate— all the meanings included within His name *al-Raḥmān*. Oftentimes what leads people to disbelieve in God and reject His existence is a misunderstanding of who He is and what His attributes and characteristics really are. If only they truly appreciated the magnificent qualities of their Creator, they would not turn away from Him. The great Companion ʿUmar ibn al-Khaṭṭāb reported that some prisoners were brought to the Prophet ﷺ, amongst whom there was a woman who was frantically running around searching for her child. When she saw the child among the captives, she

166 *Taysīr al-Karīm al-Raḥmān* 67:29, al-Saʿdī.
167 Qur'ān 3:159.

took hold of it and pressed it against her chest. The Prophet ﷺ said, "Do you think this woman would ever throw her child in fire?" They all said, "By Allāh, she would never throw the child in fire." Thereupon the Prophet ﷺ said, "Allāh is more merciful to His slaves than this woman is to her child."[168]

قُلْ أَرَءَيْتُمْ إِنْ أَصْبَحَ مَآؤُكُمْ غَوْرًا فَمَن يَأْتِيكُم بِمَآءٍ مَّعِينٍ ﴿٣٠﴾

30. Say, [O Prophet,] "If all your water were to disappear into the earth who could give you flowing water in its place?"

Sūrah al-Mulk ends on a final note of warning. Here, Allāh the Almighty instructs the Prophet ﷺ to tell his critics to consider a frightening scenario in which the very source of life, water, were to disappear into the ground,[169] such that they could not gain access to that water supply ever again.[170] In such a moment of desperation, who would they turn to for help?

This threat implies that if you continue down this path of rebellion and disbelief, the Almighty may well punish all of you in a devastating way in both this life as well as in the Afterlife. A similar verse is found in *Sūrah al-Mu'minūn*, where Allāh says: '*We send down rain from the sky in perfect measure, causing it to soak into the earth. And We are surely able to take it away*'.[171] Furthermore, this concluding verse can be said to be drawing upon the meaning of the previous one, which stressed upon the reader the importance of placing complete trust and reliance upon Allāh: *Say, [O Prophet,] "He is the Lord of Mercy—we believe in Him, and in Him [alone] we trust.*[172]

168 *Ḥadīth, Ṣaḥīḥ Muslim* 2754.

169 It is reported that Ibn 'Abbās interpreted the words *ghawran* to mean 'entered into the ground'. See: *Tafsīr Fatḥ al-Qadīr* 67:30, al-Shawkānī.

170 *Baḥr al-'Ulūm* 67:30, al-Samarqandī.

171 Qur'ān 23:18.

172 *Al-Tafsīr al-Kabīr* 67:30, al-Rāzī.

The words **disappear into the earth** is translating *ghawr,* which refers to a well when it becomes depleted and the bucket used to draw up water comes back empty.[173] In the Arabic language, we find that instead of using a verb to describe the water disappearing, the verbal-noun is used as it imparts a more emphatic meaning. This is as if to say, imagine if your drinking were to completely vanish.

The word 'flowing' translates *maʿīn,* which is understood by some to mean "clear" or "sweet" water,[174] while others have said it refers to water that appears on the surface of the earth which is easily accessible to people.[175] The obvious implication behind the words **who could give you flowing water in its place?** is that no one except Allāh has that kind of ability. Hence, people should recognise, show gratitude, and worship Him alone. Imām al-Qurṭubī also points out that in spite of all the reverence that the polytheists of Makkah showed their false gods, they knew deep down that those idols would not be able to help them in such a scenario.[176] In fact, if their instinctive response to such a question was 'only Allāh could', then they should seriously consider the absurdity of worshiping others besides Him who are incapable of saving them.[177] A similar thought-provoking verse is found elsewhere in the Qur'ān: *Have you considered the water you drink? Is it you who bring it down from the clouds, or is it We Who do so?*[178]

Reflection

The Qur'ān will often use the image of rainfall as an allusion to the source of all worldly blessings. God's removal of water can thus be taken as an allusion to removing all His blessings or the blessing of life itself. Such a threat would have resonated with the Arabs of Makkah

173 *Al-Taḥrīr wa Al-Tanwīr* 67:30, Ibn ʿĀshūr.
174 *Jāmiʿ al-Bayān fī Ta'wīl al- Qur'ān* 67:30, Imām al-Ṭabarī.
175 *Al-Taḥrīr wa Al-Tanwīr* 67:30, Ibn ʿĀshūr.
176 *Al-Jāmiʿ li-Aḥkām al-Qur'ān* 67:30, by al-Qurṭubī.
177 *Al-Tafsīr al-Kabīr* 67:30, al-Rāzī.
178 Qur'ān 56:68-69.

who lived in a desert environment where water was already scarce. In fact, the main source of fresh water they had at the time of the Prophet ﷺ was the famous well of Zamzam, the origins of which go back to the father of monotheism, Abraham, a man of God. Thus they were, as circumstances would have it, already aware that God Himself was providing them water through a Divine miracle, without which they and their forefathers, who they prided themselves on, would seize to exist. The threat within this verse was perhaps alluding to this historical fact.

Contrasting the threat in the previous verse with this verse, Imām al-Ālūsī explains that this verse is more severe than the previous one[179] and it ends the passage, as well as the entire *sūrah*, on a climactic note, leaving the reader in awe of the Almighty.

Perfect Symmetry

Verses 28 and 30 speak of the punishment of Allāh in an all-encompassing manner. Either it will come in the Afterlife or in this life. This leaves no way out for the stubborn disbeliever. The moment when they will have to face the consequences of their decisions is inevitable and unavoidable. However, the path to salvation is detailed in the middle, sandwiched in between these two verses. As mentioned in verse 29: 'Say, "He is the Lord of Mercy—in Him [alone] we believe, and in Him [alone] we trust.' The pattern of pain-salvation-pain, with survival wedged in the middle, illustrates that the only way out is through faith and submission.

179 *Rūḥ al-Maʿānī fī Tafsīr al-Qur'ān al-ʿAẓīm wa'l-Sabʿ al-Mathānī* 67:30, by al-Ālūsī.

Figure 11: The pattern of pain-salvation-pain as depicted in verses 28-30

The Beginning and End

The final verse ties in perfectly with the beginning of the *Sūrah* as the first verse declared Allāh to be the King and the universe His kingdom. A truly powerful king has total control over his subjects, and nothing expresses dominance like being able to control access to the most basic necessities upon which life depends, namely, water. Furthermore, the Prophet ﷺ established a link between water and the Kingship of Allāh when he said, 'His throne rests upon the water'.[180] Therefore, the *Sūrah* beautifully ties the beginning with its ending, making the whole message revolve around Allāh's Divine majesty, power, and magnificence.

180 *Ḥadīth, Ṣaḥīḥ Muslim* 2654.

Conclusion

This book is only a small effort to inspire further interest in engaging in a more meaningful reading of the Qur'ān. It is an attempt to make the Book of Allāh and some of the classical commentaries accessible to a wider Western audience.

During the course of my research and writing, I have tried to highlight the nuances of the Qur'ān's language and word choice; its use of Classical Arabic grammatical and rhetorical devices; its use of imagery, figures of speech, and parables; the structure and coherence of the *Sūrah* and, more importantly, the universal lessons and teachings it seeks to communicate to humanity.

Sūrah al-Mulk is replete with beautiful elements of peace and serenity that are strongly contrasted with verses of warning and punishment, making it a gripping read.

Ultimately, a study of the entire Qur'ān should be a life-long goal for every Muslim. This magnificent Book challenged and transcended the rich literary tradition of Arabia. In only two decades, it transformed a people boasting of no civilization, who were divided into perpetually warring tribal factions and devoted to a pantheon of deities, into a monotheistic civilization, which in only a century would become the largest and most prosperous in the medieval world, stretching from Spain to India, distinguished by its values, traditions, scholarship, and advancements in the arts and sciences. This is amongst the many reasons why the Qur'ān deserves to be studied and made into a life-long companion.